D1242966

EVERYBODY'S
WEAVING
BOOK

by ALFRED ALLAN LEWIS

by JULIENNE HALLEN KRASNOFF

EVERYBODY'S WEAVING BOOK

by ALFRED ALLAN LEWIS

with JULIENNE KRASNOFF

Black-and-white photography by
JULIENNE KRASNOFF

Color photography by
RONALD FRANK

Line drawings by
TAMARA HESLEN

MACMILLAN PUBLISHING CO., INC.
New York

Macmillan Publishing Co., Inc.
866 Third Avenue, New York, N.Y. 10022
Collier Macmillan Canada, Ltd.

Library of Congress Cataloging in Publication Data
Lewis, Alfred Allan.
  Everybody's weaving book.
  Bibliography: p.
  Includes index.
  1. Hand weaving. I. Krasnoff, Julienne, joint author. II. Title.
TT848.L48   746.1′4   75-31512
ISBN 0-02-571270-5

First Printing 1976

Book designed by Margaret Dodd

Printed in the United States of America

CONTENTS

INTRODUCTION

"Everybody's weaving," she said happily. Somehow I doubted it. Rachel Knopf was a charming lady and not ordinarily given to hyperbole, but she was also the Executive Director of the Handweavers Guild of America and, I thought, just a little carried away by her own enthusiasm. We were both at a craft fair which, for some quaint reason, was being conducted in a large pit in front of the McGraw-Hill Building in the busiest part of New York City. As a herd of sheep were stopping traffic on the Avenue of the Americas on their way to being shorn for the spinners, she suggested that I write a book on weaving making use of some of the facilities of the Guild.

The Handweavers Guild of America was founded by Garnette Johnson, a remarkable woman who not so many years ago looked around and saw a burgeoning textile craft movement with almost 300 community groups but no national organization, no means of communication, of getting it all together, of exchanging ideas and setting up standards. She formed a Board of Advisors composed of some of the finest weavers in the country and started publishing a quarterly magazine, *Shuttle, Spindle, & Dyepot,* which was to be distributed to the members of the newly formed Guild.

In almost no time, the weaving scene changed. Communications were opened. The HGA membership skyrocketed. It ran the gamut of textile craftsmen and craftswomen from novices to hobbyists to professionals, from spinners to dyers to art weavers to utilitarian weavers, from staid matrons to former Army officers to young commune dwellers swapping faded jeans for homespuns, from serious fabric sculptors to doily doodlers.

Rachel's original idea, on that afternoon of the shearing of the sheep, was for me to do a rather esoteric work for experts, tracing the history of weaving in this country. I was at that fair demonstrating quilting techniques taught in my book *The Mountain Artisans Quilting Book,* but I had no idea how to make the fabric I was using. "Thanks, but that's not for me," I said. "It would be like racing Mark Spitz before learning how to float. I don't even know a warp from a woof."

"Weft," she murmured.

"Exactly!" Before I could so much as contribute a piece to *Shuttle, Spindle, & Dyepot,* I would have to go through the basic act of learning how to weave. I explained that I didn't mind doing a primer on weaving, a book that really started at the beginning and took no previous knowledge for granted. My greatest value as a writer of craft books had always been not my expertise, but my initial ignorance. I'd always had to start with the very first step for the simple reason that I did not yet know the second step. The premise had been that I would work with people who could teach me. I felt without any false modesty that if I could learn a craft, *anybody* could learn it.

The idea of doing a book on weaving lingered after the day was over. I began to look through the books available for beginners. As I suspected, they were all written by experts. By definition, an expert is somebody who knows just about all there is to know in his or her field. By practice, they often assume that the reader also knows something. My problem was a familiar one for the newcomers. I knew absolutely nothing except that I wanted to know something about the craft.

These books generally fell into one of two categories (the worst of them into both). They either began with lengthy histories of weaving, or they began with lessons. Either way, they were a bit formidable for the initiate in the craft. Many of the histories were both well written and informative, but they were of little practical use to me. I really wasn't interested in learning how they wove thousands of years ago in the Tigris-Euphrates Valley. I wanted to learn how they weave today, using all of today's time- and labor-saving equipment.

The lesson books were equally frustrating. They seemed to be written in a foreign language. It was like trying to read Spanish before one had mastered any of the vocabulary.

Weaving is one of the oldest crafts and over its long history it has developed a terminology of its own. This has to be learned before one can begin to understand those books. To make matters worse, there are sometimes two words for the same thing: woof or weft, thread or yarn, end or thread, web or fabric, section or bout, selvedge or selvage, lease or section sticks, tabby or plain weave, bobbin or spool, and so on.

Most of these books come with glossaries which are much too long and broad for the beginner to attempt to memorize. Pictures of essentials would be much better. Call it what you will, this is what it looks like, and this is what it does or means. What good are unfamiliar names to somebody looking at a loom for the first time? The student wants to know what that thing-a-ma-jig is and its purpose. A name in print alone won't help: only a picture will give the information. Those first books I tried to read made me decide that if I ever did a book on weaving it would have a photographic glossary. If the reader is confused by something on the loom or in the weaving or warping, he or she should be able to thumb through the book for a picture. It is only after the identification is made that the name should be committed to memory. That is our premise in this book.

About a month after the craft fair, Rachel Knopf telephoned to ask if I was still interested in doing a primer on weaving. I replied that I was but that before anything else I had to find somebody who could both teach and do. Her response was to bring Julienne Krasnoff around to meet me. This book began with that introduction, for Julienne is indeed a superlative weaver who has also conducted very successful workshops on the subject.

Julienne agreed that there was a very real need for a book that was in itself both teacher and text. There was only one way that this could be successfully accomplished and that was with hundreds of step-by-step photographs of every facet of weaving from draft to warp to web. Five highly regarded craft books had reinforced my original belief that only photographs can teach. Drawings may explain, but they cannot substitute for physical contact with an instructor. That vital replacement can only be made by a photograph of a real hand working with real objects. It is that extra human dimension that visually proves that a person actually can do what a sketch only suggests that he or she can do.

The first order of business was for Julienne to take a series of pictures of what she considered the most important steps in learning how to weave. Then I asked every question that did not seem to be answered in the series. Some of my questions were so elementary that the expert in Julienne could only wonder at my apparent lack of learning skills. Pictures were taken to answer those queries.

Once all the photographs were assembled and captioned, Julienne disappeared from the scene, leaving me alone with yarns and equipment. With only the pictures as my guide, I had to read a draft, prepare a warp, put it on the loom, and weave through the large range of threading that was to be taught in the book.

I would very much like to say that it was a breeze but, unfortunately, that first time round was more like being caught in a hurricane. Starting almost at the beginning, with preparing a warp, I must have missed some basic steps: instead of something ready to go on the loom, I had a knot of Gordian proportions.

Back we went for more photographs. This happened with every problem I got into, until it could truly be said that the pictures had become an expert teacher. They were double-checked with another beginner, and they worked.

During my adventures in learning, I began to wonder about weaving. It defied all the reasons given for the popularity of the other textile crafts such as knitting, needlepoint, crocheting, embroidery, macrame, crewel, and even quilting.

Weaving is not portable: the crafter cannot easily carry it around and work at it anywhere, be it beach or plane or bus. It demands an investment in equipment before one can even start to do it. No matter what anybody might tell you, there are parts of it that are tricky and take a good deal of patience and practice to master. It is time-consuming, laborious, and occasionally just plain boring. It is also lonely. You very seldom carry your loom over to your neighbors' for a weaving bee, although this is beginning to change. Weavers' guilds are springing up everywhere, and the Handweavers Guild of America is not only getting people in touch with the guilds in their areas, but it is also getting the guilds in touch with each other. As weavers move on, they can learn about the guilds that may exist in their neighborhoods, or even about the feasibility of starting one of their own.

Still the drawbacks persisted. Why then were so many people everywhere getting into weaving? There were no rules governing who they were or where they came from. These new weavers were from every conceivable region, background, age, race, and socioeconomic stratum. What was the lure? What were the rewards?

I decided to venture out to meet the weavers, to speak to them and get to know them. Part of

teaching how to weave would be teaching why to weave.

Although there were as many individual reasons for getting into weaving as there were individuals in it, there were a few general motivations that cropped up time and again. Certainly, the broad range of things that could be made with weaving was a major factor for a great many crafters. They could make distinctive fabrics for clothes and upholstery, rugs, tapestries, free-form woven sculpture, pillows, wall hangings, blankets, curtains, and all manner of table linen right down to placemats. Whatever you do, don't overlook placemat power. There are a lot of respectable weavers who adore them above all else in life. And why not? Placemats are very easy to make and quick to finish. They are beautiful rewards to oneself and gifts for loved ones. They are also eminently saleable. The weaver in need of a little extra cash can find ready customers for a lovely set of handwoven placemats.

Speaking of money, the state of the economy is another prime motivation for the renaissance of weaving. People cannot afford to travel as much as they used to, and the desire for a craft that will travel with them has diminished. A loom doesn't take up that much space in a family room or "rec" room. Some of them are handsome enough to be displayed in the living room. These days they seem to be cropping up in every conceivable kind of room —from kitchen, to bedroom, to attic, to basement, to garage. I even know of one weaver who's found a way of making it a completely portable craft by setting it up in her trailer.

The ability to produce some income at one's craft is no negligible factor even for the modest hobbyist. The ability to make the craft pay grows in direct proportion to the growth of one's weaving skills. At first it's sufficient to earn back the cost of the materials and let the labor be of love. Later, some small value can be placed on the weaver's time and reckoned in the price of the product, be it wall hanging, stole, tote bag, or yardage. Finally, the work can become a source of real profit. I know a dentist who started weaving as a pastime. His wife wanted fabric to cover some furniture. Now, he's spending so much time filling orders that he has almost no time left for filling teeth.

The pleasure principle is another great satisfaction to be derived from weaving. It takes many forms.

There are those who get a sensual charge from handling fibers, yarns, fabrics. For others, it is the pleasure of working with one's hands to produce something beautiful. For all weavers there is the indescribable pleasure of self-expression. Once you've mastered the basics, the variations are almost endless.

This book is designed to give the reader some indication of the number of variations that can be played on one simple warp. What you do is up to you. It's been said that we are what we eat. Well, in a very real sense, what we weave is us. It's the fabric of our imagination and vision.

Last but not least, weaving is fun. Perhaps not in the sense of a game or a comedy but in the deeper sense of contentment. As one weaver put it: "When I first started I thought that I'd never master it. Told myself that it's too much like work to enjoy. But I kept at it, and it's not true anymore. I do enjoy it. It's not anywhere near as complicated as I thought. Truth to tell, it's easy. And I'm just so tickled at watching that fabric roll out of my loom. I can sit down to it with the weight of the world on my shoulders, a problem I can't seem to solve on my mind. And you know, it just disappears. I have a ball, and the solution comes as clear as the threading of the web. It's such a positive way to spend time, and it makes me feel so good. I just enjoy weaving. I really do enjoy it. I don't know any weaver who doesn't."

ALFRED ALLAN LEWIS

PREFACE

Everybody's Weaving Book is an invitation to the joys of weaving. Although there are many things in it for intermediate weavers—weaves they may not know, techniques and/or equipment they might want to learn about—it is primarily designed for the beginner, to teach without intimidation, to substitute the pleasure of accomplishment for the fear of failure. The professional or expert (alas, there's too often a difference between them) can stop reading here. This book is not encyclopedic nor does it delve into the esoterica of weaving. It is a primer, an ABC book, but if the reader follows through step-by-step to Z, there is very little that he or she will not be able to do in weaving or learn from the more advanced books with very minimal effort.

The photographic glossary is spaced through the book, so that the objects the reader learns to identify are those necessary for an understanding of the particular chapter in which they appear. The book begins with the selection of a loom, because that's where weaving begins. Most of the actual instructions are for making narrow strips with a great variety of weaves in them. These might be suitable for a luggage rack (see color photograph 1 facing page 32) or for little wall hangings (see color photograph 2 facing page 32).

In addition to the range of techniques that can be explored in these little strips, there is another excellent reason for using them for starting projects: they are done on narrow warps. Putting on a warp has probably discouraged more potential weavers than anything else. It's not that warping is difficult; it isn't. It's simply that it's a mechanical process, and that is the antithesis of the creative urge, the self-expression, that is such an integral and exciting part of weaving. The act of putting on a warp sets up a mental block that many cannot hurdle. That's why it is best to start with a simple and slender warp. Once you get the knack of warping, you'll find that it becomes more challenge than chore, and you'll want to explore the possibilities.

Now, let's get down to the ABCs of weaving—or rather the four special Ws: the Weaver (you), the Warp (the vertical strands in the loom) on which you work with the Weft (the moving, active horizontal strands) to create the Web (fabric).

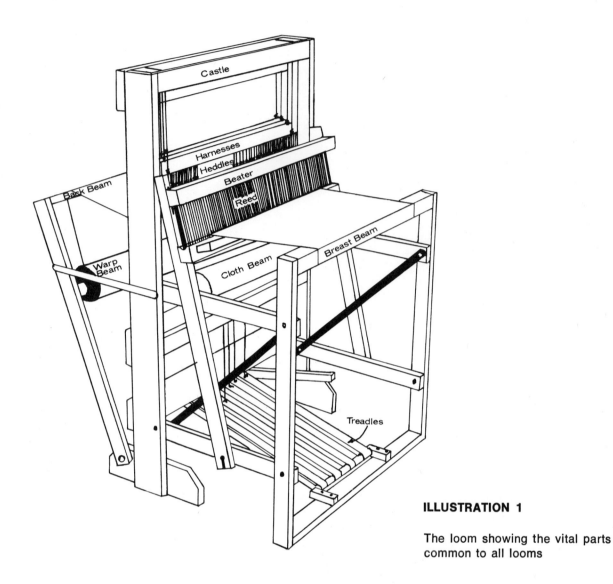

ILLUSTRATION 1

The loom showing the vital parts common to all looms

Glossary of the Loom

1 WARP BEAM The beam around which the warp is wound. A brake controls its movement. The warp goes up to the BACK BEAM.

BACK BEAM The warp is wound over the back beam and is led forward toward the harnesses in the center of the loom.

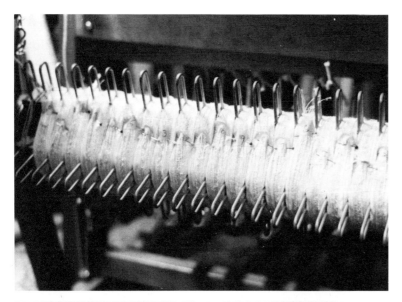

2 SECTIONAL BEAM A piece of special equipment used to put on a warp, either in place of or in conjunction with the warp beam. Because the warp is divided into sections (called "bouts"), it is especially helpful for putting on a long warp.

3 HARNESS The frame, suspended in the center of the loom, that holds the HEDDLES.

HEDDLES Made of metal or string with a hole or eye in the center through which the warp ends are brought during warping with the help of a THREADING or HEDDLE HOOK.

THREADING or HEDDLE HOOK A special instrument used to facilitate the bringing of warp ends through the heddle holes.

4 TIE-UP, LAMMS, TREADLES Attaching the LAMMS (top) to the TREADLES with cords or chains. By stepping on each TREADLE, one can govern which harnesses are put into operation.

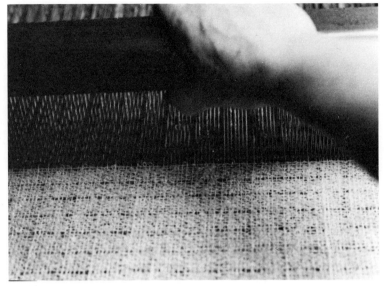

5 WEB The completed woven fabric.

BEATER The movable part of the loom used to beat the weft threads back toward the web. It holds the REED.

REED The warp is threaded through slits called "dents" and led forward toward the front beam.

6 FRONT BEAM Sometimes called the **breast beam.** The bar at the front of the loom around which the newly woven cloth goes down to the CLOTH BEAM.

CLOTH BEAM The bar around which the finished cloth is wound. Its movement is controlled by a brake.

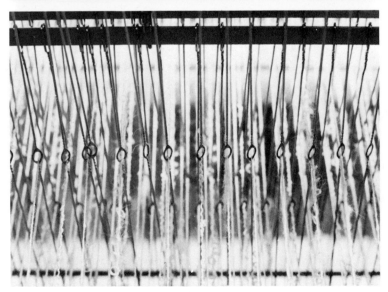

7 WARP The yarn that runs from the back of the loom through the heddles toward the front.

WARP, END, THREAD Individual strands of the warp.

8 SLEY (Noun) Also called "set." The number of warp ends per inch (EPI).

REED A comblike tool which runs the width of the weaving space of a loom and is encased in the beater. There are metal spokes at preset spaces.

DENT The space between the metal spokes of a reed. **To sley** (verb) is the act of bringing the warp ends through the dents.

SLEYING HOOK An instrument for bringing the warp ends through the dents.

SPACED WARP Pictured here, it is an arrangement of warp ends which skips some dents in the reed.

9 BOBBIN or QUILL The instrument holding the WEFT.

WEFT, FILLING MATERIAL Yarns, threads, or fibers worked horizontally through the warp to make fabric.

SHUTTLE An instrument for passing or throwing the weft through the SHED.

SHED Space in the warp created by lifting or lowering the harnesses.

WEFT THREAD, PICK, END Thread carried through the SHED by the SHUTTLE. Side-to-side horizontal thread in weaving.

10 NETTING SHUTTLE Used for sampling and for special technique for which the regular shuttle is too heavy.

SELVEDGE or SELVAGE The edge of the web. (See photograph 9.)

1 LOOMS

Fundamentally, a loom is no more than a mechanical device upon which one can weave. Weaving is no more than the interaction of vertical and horizontal threads to make cloth. The **warp** is the collective name for the vertical threads, or those threads coming toward the weaver. They are held securely in the loom. The weaver holds the horizontal threads generally, but not always, in an instrument called a **shuttle.** These threads are called the **weft** or woof. Each row of them is passed over and under the warp threads. The laced result is called the **weave** or **web.** The simplest weave is the plain or tabby weave. For the first row, the weft passes under the first thread of the warp, over the second, under the third, over the fourth, and so on. For the second row, it passes over the first, under the second, over the third, under the fourth, and so on. The third row is a repeat of the first; the fourth a repeat of the second; the fifth, the first, the sixth, the second, and so on. Endless other patterns are created by simply changing the number and order of warp threads passed over or under at any one time. Two under, one over; three under, two over, etc.

In the earliest looms, the weaver's task was to pass the weft threads under and over the warp threads by hand. This was laborious and time-consuming, not to mention terribly boring. Evenutally, probably centuries later, some unsung genius invented the **shed.** The shed did to weaving what the wheel did to transportation. The shed is the triangular space created by lifting up all the warp threads in each row to be passed under by the weft thread (or, depending on one's point of view or loom, lowering all the threads to be passed over). The weft thread is laid through the shed, automatically completing a whole row by passing over and under all the warp threads in one operation, instead of having to go in and out individual thread by thread.

"What should influence my selection of a loom?" That's one of the first questions asked by anybody seriously interested in learning how to weave. Some weavers respond in terms of the types of projects to be done, others in terms of price, still others in terms of space and portability. All these replies have validity and must play a major role in one's final selection. But one consideration is more important than any of the others—comfort. If the weaver is not comfortable at the loom, then not much weaving is going to get done. The pleasures of weaving should never be allowed to disintegrate into the misery of aching backs and arm muscles.

FRAME LOOMS

(See color photograph 3 facing page 32.)

These looms are primarily used for small projects, tapestries, wall hangings, and free weaving. They have the advantages of being portable and very inexpensive. Some may have some sort of simple shedding mechanism such as the **slot and eye rigid heddle** (See Appendix in this book). The rigid heddle also acts as a reed and beater, an advantage over frame looms without them.

To be as comfortable as possible, adjust the height and position of your chair in relation to the table on which you've set your loom.

TABLE LOOMS

(See color photograph 4 facing page 33.)

Table looms are extremely versatile. Almost all the weaving projects in this book can be done on them. They also have the great advantage of being portable and they can be set up on any table in the house. They come in a variety of weaving widths ranging from eight inches (*see photograph 12 on page 18*) to twenty-four inches (*see photograph 11 on page 18*). The eight-inch loom is primarily used for sampling, trying out different threadings that you intend to use in a larger piece to see how they look and work together. The luggage strips, discussed later, can also be made on this loom. The twenty-four-inch table looms are suitable for any projects requiring widths up to twenty-four inches.

In the table loom we are introduced to certain mechanical features that are standard in all the larger looms. First of all, there is the **warp beam** located in the back end of the loom. The warp beam enables the weaver to put on a long warp for longer projects or for several projects requiring the same warp. The mechanics of warping are fully described and illustrated in Chapter 4.

From the warp beam, the warp threads (each individual warp thread is called an **end**) are brought over the back beam to the **harnesses.** A table loom can have from two to sixteen harnesses. The more harnesses a loom has, the more weaving versatility it permits. A harness is the most important new feature to be found in the table loom.

The harnesses are frames suspended from the **castle** or superstructure of the loom. They hold the **heddles.** Depending on the weaver's finances or choice and the manufacturer's idiosyncrasies, heddles can be made of string, wire, or flat steel. The basic features they all share are that they ride freely in the harnesses and have eyes through which the warp ends can be threaded.

How do the harnesses and heddles aid the weaver? Most important, they govern the shed which, in turn, determines the weaving patterns as the rows of weft are "thrown" through it. Each row of weft is called a **pick.**

The next instrument on the table loom is the **beater.** This swings freely from the front of the loom to the castle. Its function is to beat the weft picks forward against the web.

The **reed** is encased in the beater. It is composed of a row of comblike teeth. The space between two teeth is called a **dent.** The warp ends are passed through the dents one after another from the first end to the last end. For certain weaves, dents are skipped in a given pattern. This is called "spaced warping."

The verb **to sley** is used to describe the process of passing the warp ends through the dents. To facilitate this, a **sleying hook** is a useful piece of equipment to own. The noun **sley** designates the number of warp ends per inch (**epi**) in a warp. Because it is helpful to have a reed with the same number of dents per inch as there are epi in the warp, beaters generally come with tops that can be removed so that reeds with the appropriate number of dents can be set in them.

From the reed and beater, the warp ends are brought over the **front beam** to be attached to the **cloth beam.** The cloth beam has a cloth apron, generally made of canvas, which is fastened around it. At the top of the apron is the **cloth stick.** The warp ends are tied to this rod. Both the warp and cloth beams operate on **rachets** or brakes. As the weaving progresses, the warp rachet is used to release more warp, and the cloth rachet to wind the web onto the cloth beam.

If all of this welter of terms is thoroughly confusing you, I can't say that I blame you. Don't worry about them. *This is not meant as a lesson in warping.* That comes later, in the chapter on warping, where the step-by-step photographs will make it all very clear. This is only meant as a description of the mechanical parts of looms and their functions. Even if you don't remember what it's called, the glossary will give you an idea of what it looks like and why it's there. At this point I really don't think it's very important if you confuse the terms warp beam and cloth beam, as long as you know that there are two rollers, one at the front and one at the back, and the purposes for their existence.

Now, let's get back to the four harnesses. On a table loom there is a set of corresponding levers at the side or top of the castle. The first lever raises the first harness; the second, the second harness, and so on. Raising the harness raises the warp ends, which are threaded through the heddles which are contained in it. This creates a shed through which the weft picks can pass, and that's the beginning of weaving.

The main disadvantage of the table loom is the slowness of weaving due to having to put shuttles down to operate harness levers. (Note: Rhythm *can* be built up—but it is slow.) Another disadvantage is that you are limited as far as the size and length of the project is concerned. The advantages are portability and versatility. Free from the restrictions of having harnesses tied to specific treadles, table looms are an asset when sampling and designing. This is especially true when working with more than four harnesses.

11 TABLE LOOM
(Permission of Nilus LeClerc)

12 SAMPLING TABLE LOOM
(Permission of Dick Blick)

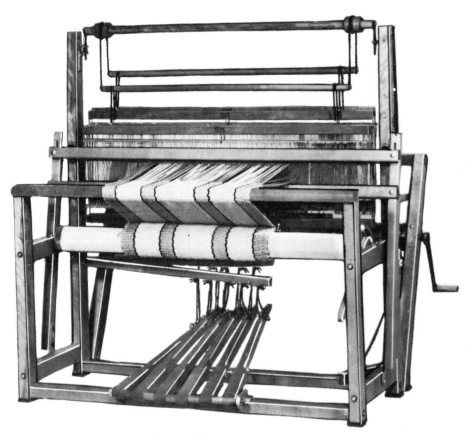

13 COUNTER-BALANCED LOOM
(Permission of Nilus LeClerc)

14 JACK LOOM
(Permission of L. W. Macomber)

15 DIRECT-ACTION LOOM
(Permission of Harrisville Looms)

16 COUNTER-MARCH LOOM
(Permission of Bexell & Son)

FLOOR LOOMS

Groping for a way to express herself beyond the lovely examples of her craft attractively displayed in her stall, a pretty and bright young weaver, exhibiting her wares at a craft fair for the first time, was trying to put her feelings about the loom into words.

"You're not weaving until you work with a floor loom. I mean you're weaving in that you're making cloth with a table loom and a frame loom. And primitive things like back straps are fun to try. But you're not *really* weaving until you get to a floor loom. Weaving is so many things from plain old tabby over here to the most esoteric combinations way out yonder. It's only with a floor loom that you can easily try them all until you find your thing."

She laughed heartily. "Maybe your thing is doing *everything*. That's great, too. As far as I'm concerned, the more harnesses the better!"

A robust man in his mid-fifties described how he got started. "It was the machine, the loom itself, the floor loom. It doesn't matter if it's Jack or counter-balanced or counter-march. It's a thing of mechanical beauty. To go back to the beginning, my wife and I had always been crafters in an amateur, hobby way. I loved woodworking and carpentry, furniture making, things like that. She tried just about everything—needlepoint, ceramics, painting. Well, about three years ago, she enrolled in this course in weaving at the local craft center. That really did it. I never saw her so excited. Weaving was it. She'd found her craft of crafts. Nothing would do but that she had her own floor loom, sixteen harnesses for openers. I was a little leery —justifiably. I'd been through about ten craft of crafts before weaving, and this one was going to take something of an investment. Sixteen-harness looms don't grow on trees, but she kept after me. She finally said, 'Make one for me. We've already got more kitchen cabinets than we have dishes and more book shelves than we have books. Make something useful. Make me a loom—if you can.' I took the bait.

"First thing was to learn how to use one, so I could see how the parts operated. I enrolled in the weaving class. I was surprised at the people at that first lesson. All kinds of people—men and women, kids and senior citizens, drop-out types, and even a college professor—and they were all hitting it off. They had this thing in common. They wanted to weave. Well it seemed to me there must be more here than meets the eye. Then I got at the loom, and that was it. Love at first sight! What a beauty of a machine that is. Spare, lean, not an extra part. Simple. Everything means something. Everything functions. None of your extra cogs and wheels to confuse the issue. Well, I built one. But we've got three more we've bought. I can't take time off from the weaving for the carpentry. We both love the weaving—have several projects going at once—but for me, first, I loved that loom."

The basic advantages of the floor looms over other looms are the flexibility in size and length of warp they permit and even more important, the **treadles.** Harnesses are raised or lowered to create sheds by pressing down on the treadles with one's feet. This leaves the weaver's hands free to control the weft and establish a rhythmic and even beat.

The **weft** or filling material is held in or wound around an instrument called a **shuttle.** When the shed is raised, the shuttle is passed or "thrown" through it, leaving the weft thread in its wake. The shed is lowered and the thread is beaten back with the beater.

With a table or rigid-heddle frame loom, this movement involves several manual operations which break the continuous flow and rhythm. Once you've thrown the shuttle, you have to put it down in order to release the shed with one hand, while the other is prepared to beat. The shed is raised again after beating and the shuttle once more taken in hand.

This all becomes one operation with a floor loom. The shed is raised and lowered with the foot. One hand controls the beater while the other holds the shuttle. Nothing has to be set down and a work rhythm can be established.

Harnesses are not usually tied directly to the treadles. Each one is attached to a moving bar called a **lamm.** The individual lamms can be attached to one or more treadles. Attaching the lamms to the treadles is called the **tie-up.** It is done with chain or rope. This allows one to use many combinations of harnesses and it requires no greater mechanical effort than a shift of the foot. This is especially useful for advanced weavers.

Here is a simplification of how it works. Suppose you want to use harnesses 1 and 3 to make a shed for the first weft shot (one thread or pick passed through the shed) and then 1 and 4 for the next. The tie-up is the lamm for harness 1 and the lamm for harness 3, both linked to treadle A; the lamm for harness 1 is also linked to treadle B as is the lamm for harness 4. Then you step on treadle A for the first weft shot and treadle B for the second weft shot. Once the tie-ups are made, that is all that needs to be done to change the shed to create the most intricate webs.

Floor looms come in three varieties: the counter-balanced, the Jack, and the counter-march.

COUNTER-BALANCED LOOMS

(See photograph 13 on page 19.)

The counter-balanced loom comes with an even number of harnesses. The harnesses are tied in pairs to rollers. When you step on a treadle, one harness goes down, and its partner goes up, thus creating the shed. In the four harness looms the tie-up can be such that a pair of harnesses lower, while the opposite pair rises.

Because the warp stretches in a straight line from the front of the loom to the rear, very little pressure is put on it. This makes the counter-balanced loom the choice of those who like to work with delicate fibers or wools. Another big plus is its price. Because it is so simple to construct, the counter-balanced loom is usually less expensive than other types of looms.

The disadvantage of the counter-balanced loom is that it is unable to weave a pattern that calls for three harnesses working against one, as in the double weave *(see Chapter 6)*. Some of these looms can be equipped with a shedding device to overcome this shortcoming, but it is an additional piece of equipment and an additional expense.

JACK LOOMS

(See photograph 14 on page 19.)

Jack looms are the most versatile of all looms and the type most in use in the United States. They come equipped with four or more harnesses. Many are constructed so that the additional harnesses can be added as the weaver feels the need for them. In this sense, the loom can grow as the crafter's skills grow.

The Jack loom is a rising-shed loom (most table looms are also Jack looms). Each harness works independently of the others. When the treadle is depressed, the harnesses rise according to the pattern in which the lamms are tied up to it.

The direct-action loom *(see photograph 5 on page 20 and color photograph 6 facing page 33)* is an inexpensive adaptation of the Jack loom. Manufacturing costs are lower for the direct-action loom because the lamms are eliminated and each harness is tied directly to a treadle. These looms present no problems when only four harnesses are in operation. By using both feet, any combination of harnesses can be raised at the same time.

The disadvantage of the Jack loom is that the warp is held down under constant tension. This can present a problem when working with delicate fibers.

COUNTER-MARCH LOOMS

(See photograph 16 on page 20.)

The counter-march loom combines the characteristics of the counter-balanced and the Jack looms. There are two sets of lamms. The harnesses that are to rise are tied to one set, while all of the other harnesses are tied to the other.

The counter-march loom is generally large and equipped with an overhead beater. The combination of this with rising and sinking harnesses make it the least tiring to use and the favorite of production weavers. Because of the firm beat of the overhead beater, it is also a good choice for rug weaving.

One of its major drawbacks is its size. Another is certainly the complicated tie-ups. The fact that you can step on only one treadle at a time presents still another disadvantage for experimental weavers.

Most types of floor looms are available in small versions. They lack the sturdiness of the larger models, but they are perfectly adequate if space is limited or if the weaver intends to travel with a loom.

Most floor looms have two more treadles than harnesses (*i.e.,* six treadles on a four-harness loom).

The extra two treadles are reserved for tie-ups for the **plain or tabby shed.**

Before selecting a loom, the weaver should try as many models as possible. Even if no store in your area stocks them, there's bound to be a school or craft center that has some. Weavers are generally great zealots for their craft, and they're more than happy to let novices examine their looms on the chance that they're going to make converts.

You should be able to sit at your loom with your arms resting on the breast beam in a relaxed position and your feet comfortably reaching the treadles. Your size in relation to the size of the loom and the height of the loom bench forms the ratio of comfort.

Next to comfort, the construction of the loom is the most important consideration. Even if you're a total beginner, you should satisfy yourself that all the following requirements are met (whether or not the jargon means anything to you!): The loom should be made of a hard wood and sturdily put together. The brakes controlling the cloth and warp beams should hold for the hardest beats. This is especially important in rug weaving. If it is a rachet and pawl brake, the pawl should drop into place as soon as pressure is removed from the release. Although a friction brake is easier to adjust, the cables sometimes do slip. They must be tested.

Be proud of being a beginner. You're embarking on a great new adventure. Study the pictorial glossary accompanying this chapter. Ask every question you can think of about the workings of all the parts of your loom. Five minutes of badgering can save years of regret and frustration.

A weaver can spend a lifetime exploring the possibilities of a two-harness loom. A four-harness loom is better, however, and an eight is better than that. There's no law saying you have to use all of the harnesses, but they're nice to have in case you get involved in a more complicated weaving passion later.

Get the widest loom you can afford and house. You don't have to use the entire width for every project. There are many weavers working three-inch warps on sixty-inch looms, but there are no weavers who can possibly work a sixty-inch warp on a three-inch loom. The greater the width, the greater possibilities.

Heddles may be made of string, wire, or flat steel.

The string are quieter and lighter, the wire cheaper than flat steel. There are no "best" selections. It's a matter of personal preference, availability, and economics.

As a rule, chain tie-ups are easier to use than cord tie-ups, but they are also noisier. The selection is as much a matter of one's sensitivity to sound as anything else.

A second back beam with a second warp beam is good to have in reserve for certain types of weaving. If that second warp beam is a sectional beam, that's best of all. It makes long warps so much easier to mount.

Our recommendation for a loom is an eight-harness Jack loom with two warp beams (one a sectional), two back beams, chain tie-ups, flat steel heddles (or wire with solid eyes), a width of forty-five to sixty inches, and a bench with an adjustable seat. If price turns this ideal loom into a dream, then settle for the best reality that you can find.

Shop around. The suppliers' directory at the end of this book lists several sources. Send for the catalogues and study them. The best way to select a loom is to try out as many as you can find. It's a case of a trial saving many errors. The loom you choose should be, like most choices in life, the one you love. If your loom turns out to be a thirty-inch, four-harness counter-balanced loom with cord tie-ups, string heddles, and no sectional beam, forget everything we've said. That's the loom for you. Enjoy it.

2 YARNS, THREADS, AND FIBERS

She was a very attractive young girl in her mid-twenties. There was a marvelous richness to the textures of the woven bags that she was exhibiting at the craft fair. We asked how she'd got into weaving.

"I think I just liked the touch of the materials. The fabrics, and yarns, and fibers said something very special to me. I'd tried many crafts at school, you know, but I just had this feeling for the materials involved in weaving that I never got from anything else. I mail-order for samples all over the world. And every time I find something new, I get a new charge. I keep a file on lots of companies selling yarns. Samples. I update the pricing once a year. It's a lot of paper work, but it's necessary. Besides, I love going through those files every now and then and reminding myself by touch of the wonderful possibilities and projects suggested by various threads."

At another booth a young man was doing very well with yardage of his own design. He said: "Silk, linen, wool, cotton, some of the synthetics—their textures all say different things. Just from fingering them, whole designs can pop into my head."

She was no longer young, but there was a likeable vitality to her. She had been a fairly successful painter and the feeling for color showed in her work. She said: "Weaving just seems a natural extension of my painting. When I first got curious about it, I wasn't sure I was really involved until after I visited this terrific yarn store. It knocked me out. All those colors. As a painter, I always used a vivid pallette. And I looked around. Those yarns, those delicious colors—they were all over, surrounding me. Not just on a board in front of me. Everywhere. It was like living in color. I just had to mix them up, to work with them, to get my hands on them. I knew that I was going to become the best damned weaver I knew how to be. It was the yarns that told me so. They still do."

For some, it's the challenge of the loom that creates the weavers. For others, it's the yarns. Touch is one of the subtlest of the five senses. Touch, feel, feeling. Their feeling for the craft is truly tactile: It comes from the touch of the materials.

Sight is the other sense that responds strongly to fabric. Color and texture are the two things that attract or repel in fabric. The wonderful challenge in weaving is that one can experiment with both. It's all in how one mixes and blends the basic materials in the weave. These threads, yarns, and fibers can be as fine as angel's hair or coarse as cord; they can be their natural color or dyed more tints and hues than ever striped a rainbow; they can be satin smooth to the touch or as rough hewn and woody as native bark. Or they can be eclectic combinations of all, the sugar and spice, sweet and pungent of an exotic weaving "recipe."

Whether it is the loom itself, or the blend of weft and warp, or the sensory perceptions of yarn, thread, and fiber that attracts one to weaving, it is necessary to become familiar with the available materials. The best way to do this is to send to the yarn companies for samples. (There is a list of them in the suppliers directory at the back of the book.) This will give an indication of accessibility, variety, colors, prices, and yardage counts. Study your samples. Start a file on what is around and what it costs and constantly keep it up-to-date.

The basic materials used by handweavers are the natural ones: cotton, wool, linen, silk. In other words, plant and animal products. For the purposes of simplicity, let's arbitrarily define them in this book. **Yarn** is what we'll call the spun by-products of quadrupeds (sheep, llama, camel, vicuna, alpaca, etc.). **Thread** will delineate those materials spun from a plant or insect (cotton, flax, silk worm, etc.). **Fibers** will be the man-made products (nylon, orlon, dacron, etc.). The latter are becoming increasingly available. Many are perfect simulations of natural products. It is often impossible to tell by look or touch that they are not the real thing. What's still more pleasant is that they are often in greater supply and at lower prices than the genuine article.

Different yarns and threads have different tensile strengths even when they come from the same source such as cottons or wools. They shrink and stretch at different rates. Until you become familiar with these materials and their singularities, it is best to confine experiments to color and reserve texture for later projects.

The novice weaver's first project should be woven of the same material in both warp and weft or, at most, one in warp and only one other in weft. This will still allow great fun and experimentation in working color and design.

There are standard measurements for some materials, making it possible to determine the

amount or length of strands by knowing the size and weight of the allotment. Other materials must be figured either from supplier's information or by personal measuring. Another thing to bear in mind in measuring or determining the amount of material necessary for a given project is that "singles" refers to one strand of a given yarn, thread, or fiber and "plies" to two or more strands twisted together (*i.e.,* two-ply is two strands, three-ply, three, etc.).

COTTON

There are standard measures for the weight of cotton, which makes it very simple for the weaver to determine how much he or she may need for a given project. The **gauge** of the thread is given numerically: the higher the number, the finer it is. The heaviest thread is #1 cotton. There are 840 yards to the pound of single-ply. The yardage per pound in each number is ascertained by multiplying 840 by that number. #2 is two times 840 or 1,680 yards. #10, therefore, has 8,400 yards per pound. This refers only to single-ply and would be marked as follows: 2/1 or 10/1. The first number gives the gauge and the second is the ply.

10/2 cotton would be a two-ply #10 cotton. To find the yardage per pound of plied cotton, multiply 840 by the first number and divide by the second. 10/2 has 8,400 divided by two, or 4,200 yards per pound. 10/3 would be 8,400 divided by three or 2,800 yards per pound.

MERCERIZED COTTON

Mercerized cotton has been processed to be stronger, have more luster, and be more colorfast than its unmercerized cotton sister. It is an excellent choice for one's first warps. 3/2 perle (a mercerized thread) set as twelve ends per inch (epi) or 5/2 at fifteen epi are both suitable for most projects.

WOOL AND WORSTED

Wool and worsted both come from the fleece of sheep. The difference is in the preparation for spinning. Worsted is spun from the longest strands and is very strong. It is particularly good for making fabric for upholstery and men's suits, where hard finish and long wear are the desirable characteristics.

Wool is spun from the shorter strands and makes a softer yarn well suited for weaving fabrics for women's apparel, scarves, and blankets.

The bad news about wool is that its measurements have never been completely standardized. One must rely on the supplier's information as to length. For this reason it is advisable to label it with the information when you buy it and to keep your sample file absolutely accurate so you can reorder.

Although there is no overall system, there are several measurements that have become recognized among dealers. Among these are **cut, run,** and **worsted:**

· Cut contains 300 yards per pound of #1.
· Run contains 1,600 yards per pound of #1.
· Worsted contains 560 yards per pound of #1.

With these base figures, gauges and plies are reckoned as they are with cotton.

LINEN

Linen is the thread spun from the stems of the flax plant. (These slender, erect annuals with delicate, blue blosoms yield a lovely natural dye and also have seeds which give us linseed oil.) Linen is measured by the old European yarn or thread measure of the **lea.** It is usually 80 yards for a lea of wool, 120 yards for silk or cotton, and 300 yards for linen. A pound of #1 lea linen is also 300 yards. Gauges and plies are reckoned as with cotton.

There are several varieties of linen. The names indicate the way in which they have been treated during and after spinning.

• **Line** linen thread is spun from the longest strands of the stem. The shorter fibers are spun into *tow* threads and are less sturdy.

• **Wetspun** linen is passed through hot water during the spinning process. The result is a smooth thread suitable for weaving clothing, table cloths, or any other fabrics in which a "sheen" is desired. They make excellent warps.

• **Dryspun** has a softer, fuzzy finish. A single dryspun thread is not suitable for use in a warp because the thread is so delicate. Although lacking in strength, it does make a good weft thread. Dryspun threads have great absorbency, and the plied variety (a 10/2 for instance) can be woven into very good towelling. Plied dryspun threads can also be used for warps.

• **Gillspun** linen is spun in a manner that strengthens the threads, making it especially adaptable to rugged use.

• **Polished linen** has a starch solution added in the spinning. This fortifies delicate threads so that they will not break during weaving.

One last note on linen: fabrics woven of it have to be "finished." This means that they must be washed and pressed with a very hot iron while still damp.

SILK

Silk is measured by the old French unit of the **denier** (the amount bought in medieval times by the obsolete coin of the same name). Unlike other thread or yarn measures, the higher the number of a silk thread, the heavier it is. For example, #1 has 4,464,528 yards per pound and #10 has one tenth rather than ten times that amount per pound (446,452.80 yards). These low numbers are quite meaningless for weavers. #50 denier is still considered exceedingly fine, and #900 denier (which yields 4,950 yards per pound) quite practical.

Raw silk is the thread as it is unreeled from the silk cocoon. Until the processor has boiled it, it is coated with a gummy substance. **Tussah** silk is gathered from wild silk cocoons. **Douppioni** is a nubby thread spun from the short strands.

When short strands of silk are added to other yarns and threads to give them luster and special qualities, they are called **noils.** A spun silk noil is a very heavy thread which yields 840 yards per pound.

SYNTHETICS

In the realm of fibers, man is getting more and more adept at imitating nature. New man-made fibers that simulate natural threads and yarns are being introduced everyday. But the appearance of truth is not always the actuality of it. With synthetics, manufacturers' labels and instructions must be very carefully checked. What appears to be a washable yarn or thread may not be washable at all and they should not be used for weaving fabric articles like place mats, which you may want to throw into the washing machine. To save frustration and time, check those fibers bearing in mind the purposes you want them to serve.

KNITTING YARNS

Knitting yarns are much more expensive than weaving yarns. Sometimes they are so exciting in color or texture that the price becomes no object; at other times their ready availability more than compensates for the higher price. Generally speaking, the weaver does much better staying with products that are designed for weaving.

In addition to cost, knitting yarns have other drawbacks. They have a much looser twist than their weaving counterpart and should be used for a warp only with extreme care. Novelty yarns with large slubs (nubby bumps) may not pass through the heddles and reed. Test them before going to the trouble of making a warp. The novelty and knitting yarns do make excellent wefts and can be used to create a wonderful effect when used with a sturdy warp.

MILL ENDS

In these days in which we're all more than a little economy conscious, mill ends are marvelous bargains for those who don't mind taking a few extra pains.

Frequently, textile factories offer surplus yarns to handweavers at reduced rates. They are usually available through weaving supply houses which buy them from mills in bulk quantities. Keep checking your dealers for them. Even if you have no immediate use for them, the price may be so right that it pays to put them away for future projects.

The drawback is that the mill ends are often unlabeled and the purchaser has to play detective.

That's when your file comes in very handy. These yarns, threads, and fibers can be compared to your samples of known materials, and their statistics can be determined or at least estimated with a fair degree of accuracy.

Without a file you'll just have to measure by hand. With or without a file, it's a good idea to test all mill ends for washability and color fastness.

Upon receiving a shipment of any yarns, threads, or fibers that are not being used immediately, you should fasten a tag listing all the vital statistics to the cone or skein. When you do get around to using it, this will give you all the information at a glance.

After learning all the secrets of your loom, become intimate with the materials. A love affair with weaving often begins with a passion for a piece of yarn. Keep as much as possible on hand, so you can go to work on a whim.

The following photographs give some helpful tips on how to determine what your warp is going to look like before warping and putting it on the loom.

Planning A Warp

17 Mark an index card at one-inch intervals. Fold the card in half and wind yarn around it, leaving a space the width of the yarn between each turn. The number of turns per inch indicates the number of warp ends per inch of warp (epi). Colors can be planned at the same time by using different colored yarns in the turns.

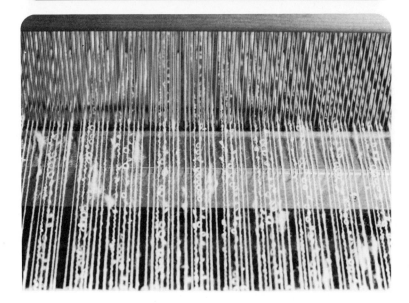

18 After wrapping the folded index card, weave with a needle threaded with weft yarn. By doing this for one inch, it will indicate the number of weft ends per inch in the weave. It will also allow you to check the interaction of color.

Spaced Weaving

19 Seven different yarns were threaded here in an eight-dent reed with every eighth dent skipped. Threaded on a four-harness loom, the odd number of warp ends shifts from harness to harness, adding interest in the character of the fabric.

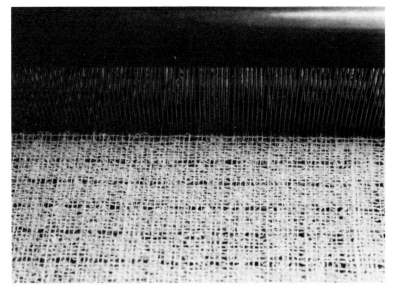

20 Repeating the same sequence of yarns in the weft (including the space) produces an interesting fabric texture.

21 The seven different yarns are piled together and wound on one shuttle producing a very heavy weft end. (See color photo 8 facing page 64.)

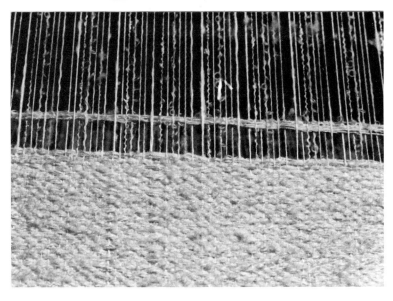

22 The seven-ply yarn is woven on the seven-yarn warp to produce a heavy fabric.

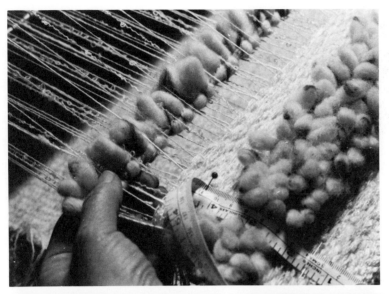

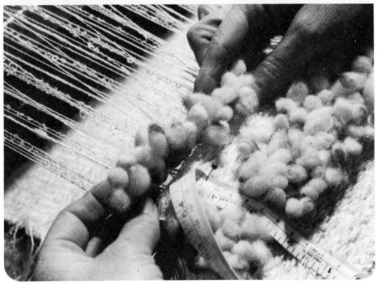

23 and 24 Novelty weft yarns can be woven and beaten into the warp by hand. They make a marvelous trim on a pillow made of the seven-ply yarn in a plain weave. (See color photo 9 facing page 64.)

3 DRAFTS, TIE-UPS, TREADLING ORDERS, DRAWDOWNS

Weavers are very fortunate people. They can speak to each other across language barriers and they can swap "recipes" for weaving patterns across national boundaries. All that's required is that you learn a few basic symbols that are becoming standard in modern books and periodicals.

Once you've got your very simple weaver's shorthand memorized, you can look at a drawdown, which is actually a picture of the weaving pattern or plan, and know exactly how it's done on the loom. Can any pastry chef do as well simply by looking at a picture of a cake?

The first step is to be able to read a **draft,** and you're about to discover that it really couldn't be easier. What's more, it's fun, almost as much fun as the weaving itself. One expert weaver put it this way: "I just love looking at the drawdowns and drafts in magazines and books. Even if I don't get around to doing them, I just love seeing how those beautiful pieces are done. If it's particularly appealing, I'll copy it out. I've got a whole book full of future projects. Someday I'm going to lock the door to my work room, and sit down with that book and let the rest of the world go by while I do them all. Until then, I'm going right on getting pleasure out of reading those drawings."

Illustration 2 shows the symbols most commonly used in drafts. Also called a **threading plan,** the draft simply indicates how each warp end is threaded.

Figures a and b are used when the warp ends are all of one yarn or thread. The numerical system (b) further indicates the number of the harness to which the end is threaded.

Figure c indicates light- and dark-colored warp ends (D = dark, L = light) and is frequently used for double-weave drafts. (See double weave in Chapter 5.)

Figure d shows symbols used to indicate different threads, yarns, or colors in the same warp.

ILLUSTRATION 2

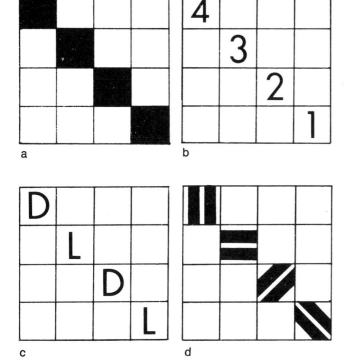

a

b

c

d

ILLUSTRATION 3

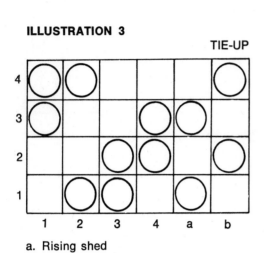

TIE-UP

a. Rising shed

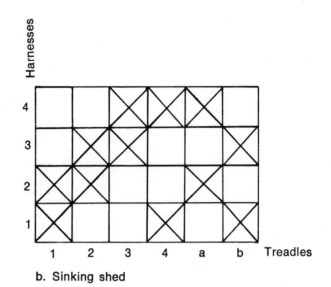

Harnesses

Treadles

b. Sinking shed

DIRECT TIE-UP

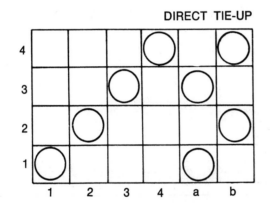

ILLUSTRATION 4

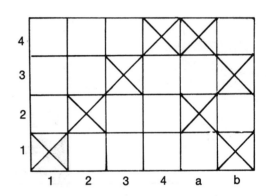

Illustration 3 diagrams the **tie-up,** that is, which harnesses are raised or lowered by each individual treadle. The numbers and letters across the bottom of the diagrams represent the treadles. The numbers running up the sides are the harnesses.

These, then, are diagrams for tie-ups on four-harness looms with six treadles in operation. In both cases, treadles a and b are for tie-ups of tabby or plain weaves.

The symbols for tie-ups on a rising-shed (Jack loom) plan will always be circles. The symbols for tie-ups on a sinking shed (counter-balanced loom) plan will always be crosses.

On the rising shed, harnesses 3 and 4 are tied to treadle 1. On the sinking shed, harnesses 1 and 2 are tied to treadle 1. *In the weaving, the result is exactly the same.*

When treadle 1 is depressed on a Jack loom,

1 Luggage rack with six strips. Over thirty weaves and weaving techniques were used in making them.

2 Wall hangings woven on same warps as strips. Includes many variations on techniques used in the strips.

3 Silver wall hangings using metallic threads in both warp and weft and jewel woven in for spectacular display of basic weaves.

4 Rigid-heddle table loom with log cabin weave on it, and resting on a log cabin cloth and rug.

5 Table loom.

6 Two-harness loom. As you can see, everybody's weaving these days.

7 Floor loom with rosepath banners on wall behind it.

harnesses 3 and 4 rise. This creates the shed. When the shuttle carrying the filling material (weft) is thrown through, the individual pick (weft thread) passes over the warp threads on harnesses 1 and 2 and under those on harnesses 3 and 4.

When treadle 1 is depressed on the counter-balanced loom, harnesses 1 and 2 sink to form the shed, and the result is still that the weft end passes over warp threads on 1 and 2 and under those on 3 and 4.

It's obvious from the diagrams that whenever a pair of harnesses rises on the Jack loom, the opposite pair sinks on the counter-balanced loom.

If the weaver should happen to tie up a Jack loom according to a counter-balanced loom diagram, the fabric will be woven in reverse. *This is nothing to worry about.* When the weaving is completed and the fabric is taken off the loom, it can be turned over and the flip side will have the desired pattern.

Illustration 4: The direct tie-up is the tie-up for the direct-action Jack loom. Regular rising and sinking shed looms can also be tied up in this manner. In both instances, the first harness is tied up to the first treadle, the second to the second, and so on. If there are two extra treadles, they are used for tabby sheds.

This is also the way a table loom would be diagrammed. Instead of treadles, there are levers. The first lever raises the first harness, and so on.

By using both feet on floor looms (or pressing multiple levers at one time on a table loom), any four-harness tie-up plan can be followed.

Let's translate the tie-ups in Illustration 3 on page 00 to direct tie-ups. For the Jack or table loom direct tie-up, one should depress treadles 3 and 4 for the first weft row (also called **weft shot**), 1 and 4 for the second, and so on. For the direct tie-up counter-balanced loom, it would be treadles 1 and 2, 2 and 3, etc. There's much to be said for direct tie-ups. They not only save the effort of retying the treadles, but they're also very good leg exercise for the weaver.

Drawdowns

A **drawdown** will show on paper how the interlacing of warp and weft will appear in the finished woven pattern. It is particularly valuable when working from an original draft, that is, a warp-threading pattern of your own design, or developing an original treadling order for a standard draft (known or traditional threading).

In working out original designs, long skips are generally to be avoided. These occur where the warp and weft do not interlace and long stretches of the same warp or weft thread are exposed. This shows up immediately in the drawdown and is much easier to change on paper, before the loom is warped, than on the actual loom.

Rosepath is a traditional threading upon which many design variations can be played. Because of its flexibility, the Craft Students League in New York City uses it to teach drafting and weave possibilities to all beginning students. *(See Chapter 6 and color photos 13-23).*

The draft for rosepath can be found at the top of *Illustration 5.* Next to it is the tie-up, including the tabby sheds, for a Jack loom. For a sinking-shed loom, simply tie-up the harnesses not filled with circles to their respective treadles (*i.e.,* harnesses 3 and 4 to treadle 1).

The threading, as indicated in the draft, is a straight progression of threads 1, 2, 3, and 4, on harnesses 1, 2, 3, and 4, then down for threads 5, 6, and 7 on harnesses 3, 2, and 1. The eighth warp end is threaded on harnesses 4, and then the threading begins all over again. Repeat this sequence until the entire warp is threaded.

Drawdowns are made on graph paper. A good scale to use is eight squares to the inch. They should have at least two repeats of the pattern unit plus whatever portion of it that is necessary to balance the weave at the selvedges.

The **treadling order** is found beneath the tie-up in Illustration 5. It quite simply indicates the order in which the treadles are used in this pattern. For the first weft shot, treadle 1 is depressed. In this tie-up, harnesses 1 and 2 are put in operation. After locating the 1 and 2 spaces on the draft, a glance at the drawdown indicates that all the squares under those numbers, in the first row, have been filled in. The same thing occurs in every row, depending on which treadle is put in action.

For a counter-balanced loom, the drawdown for this pattern would have blank squares filled in and those blacked out would be left blank.

ILLUSTRATION 5

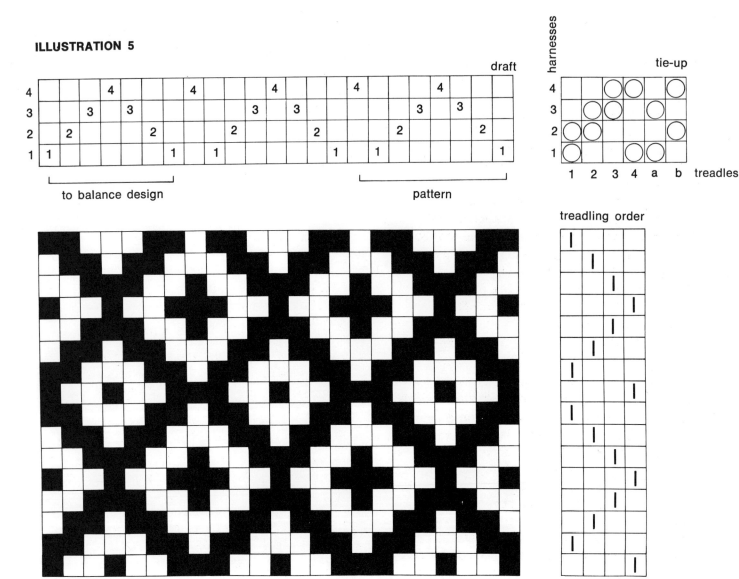

This is a good point to test yourself. Cover the drawdown in Illustration 5. Take a sheet of graph paper and, using the information in the draft, tie-up, and treadling order, do your own drawdown. If you're doing it correctly, it should be a duplicate of the one illustrated. If it isn't, check back to find the error, and make corrections.

If you turn Illustration 5 on its side, you will discover that in this particular pattern the treadling order is the same as in the draft. This is what is meant by "weave as drawn in" and the charming colonial phrase "tromp as writ," although this takes on another meaning in relation to colonial overshot (see Chapter 6).

As you can see in the photographs of pillows (*see color photographs 13 to 20*), there are a great variety of patterns that can be worked using rosepath threading. Just for fun, why not try doing some drawdowns for patterns of your own design? Keep the restrictions of tie-up and draft in mind. For example, you have no treadle that will activate harnesses 1 and 3. You cannot use them in a design without bringing in a fifth treadle and making a tie-up to those harnesses. This, of course, is unnecessary with direct tie-up. You could simply treadle 1 and 3 simultaneously. (Many four-harness looms come with two extra treadles especially for tabby.)

ILLUSTRATION 6

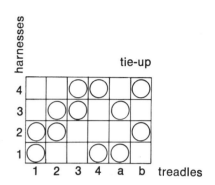

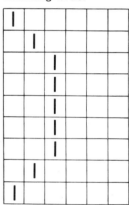

There are times when the drawdown indicates that there will be long "skips" in the weaving, such as in the elongated pattern in *Illustration 6.* There is no reason to discard the pattern if the design is a pleasing one. This is an instance in which the tabby tie-ups can prove very valuable. A Tabby shot is used between each pattern row.

In this case the treadling would be 1, a, 2, b, 3, a, 3, b, etc. Tabby shots are frequently not indicated in the treadling orders but are implied in the nature of the weave.

To make these tabby shots disappear, use a pattern weft that is heavier than the warp. Fill another shuttle with the same material as the warp. Use this for the tabby shots, and the heavier pattern wefts will cover them.

ILLUSTRATION 7

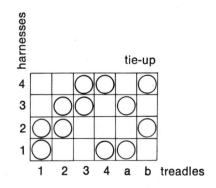

draft

harnesses   tie-up

treadling order

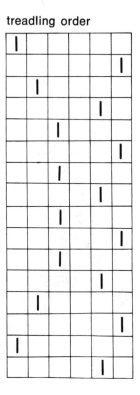

   In *Illustration 7,* the tabby shots are an integral part of the pattern and should be treated as such, which is why they appear in the treadling order.

   Drawdowns are sometimes done from the draft *before* the tie-up and treadling order. A little test will indicate how easy it is to determine the latter. Using Illustration 7, cover the tie-up and treadling order. Study the draft in relation to the drawdown. It is obvious that harnesses 1 and 2 are used in row 1. This is the tie-up for the first treadle. Tabby shots are always obvious because every other square is blacked out.

   Another interesting thing about patterns and drawdowns can be discerned by looking at Illustration 6 and Illustration 7. The weaves look very different and yet the only change in the patterns is the addition of the alternating tabby shots in the same weft material. Those permanent tabby tie-ups come in so handy. Because of this, the weaver should always try to reserve two treadles for them.

   One last note: it is easier to read from the top to the bottom of a page. Therefore, we do a draw*down.* However, one weaves *up.* The first weft shot is always the bottom of the web or woven piece. To get a true look at what the finished work is going to look like, turn the drawdown upside down.

Warping Glossary

25 CHAIN (Verb) To remove the warp from the warping board. (Noun) Warp prepared for putting on a loom.

WARPING BOARD Pegged frame used in making a warp.

26 BOBBIN and SPOOL WINDER Piece of equipment for winding yarn, thread, or fiber onto spool or bobbin (pin which holds filling material in shuttle).

YARDAGE COUNTER Device for keeping track of the length of yarns, threads, and fibers.

THREAD CLIPPER Special scissors for cutting threads, yarns, and fibers.

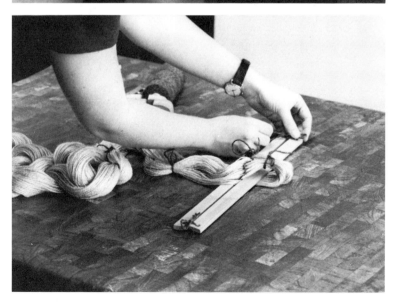

27 LEASE STICKS Sticks put through a warp chain to keep the threading cross while the warp is being put on the loom.

28 HORIZONTAL WARPING REEL Special equipment. A reel used for making a warp.

29 RADDLE A bar studded with pins used to spread the warp evenly across the back beam. After the warp is spread, masking tape is used to seal the pins.

30 SPOOL RACK Device used for holding spools when using multiple strands in warping.

PADDLE Implement for keeping strands separated in multiple-strand warping.

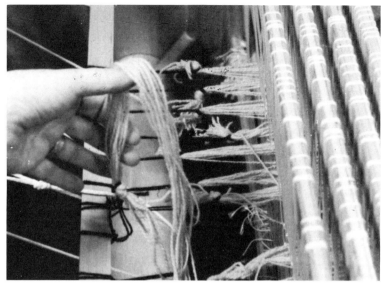

31 THRUMS Yarn left at end of warp that cannot be woven.

32 UMBRELLA SWIFT Holds skeins of yarn.

BALL WINDER Used for making balls of yarn.

33 WARPING BOARD (small) Suitable for making warps for rigid-heddle looms and short projects, it makes a warp up to 4½ yards long.

34 WEAVER'S KNOT Used for tying on new warps and repairing warp ends. Make loop at the end of warp end, bring second strand up through it, around and over loop ends, and under itself. Tighten.

Preparing Harnesses Before Putting on a Warp

35 If more heddles are needed on a harness for a particular warp, transfer the additional heddles by stringing both top and bottom holes on a piece of florist (or similar) wire. Slide the harnesses off the wire and onto the heddle bars in the harness.

36 If there are surplus heddles on a harness and you don't want to remove them, slide them to one side of the harness and tie them together with a piece of string. This will prevent them from interfering with the warp.

4 WARPING

One of the best weaving teachers on the West Coast gave the message on warping in very simple terms. She said: "To me, the basic element in learning to weave is learning how to warp simply and directly so that your warp is not going to be something that makes it more difficult for you to learn what's happening."

For some reason warping is so terrifying to a great many beginners that it stops them from going any further in the exploration of a craft that is potentially so pleasurable. There's no actual reason for this fear. It's a simple mechanical process that anyone can master. In classes all over the country, there are pre-teen children who are putting on excellent warps with no problems.

One should always bear in mind the creative possibilities of even the most basic steps. One prize-winning weaver said: "I'm going to spend seventeen years of my life exploring tabby. You don't really have to know more than tabby."

The teacher quoted above agreed. "My work is almost all from the tabby or twill families, and it pleases me, and it seems to please many other people. You can space it, change the size of it, use thick and thin contrasts. It just goes on forever."

When a weaver speaks of putting on a good warp, what is meant by it? It is no more than putting on one that is evenly tensioned so that the weaving goes smoothly and the web has a firm and consistent body. The necessity for this cannot be overemphasized, for the finished product is going to depend upon it.

There are many easy ways to put a warp on a loom. Several of them are going to be discussed in this book. (The sectional method requires special equipment which can be ordered with the loom.) The beginner should try them all. The way that is best for each weaver will only become apparent after many new warps are made and mounted.

The first projects are actually six sample strips. They have been planned to serve as straps on a luggage rack *(see color photograph 1 facing page 32)* but the same warps can be used to weave small hangings *(see color photographs 2 and 3 facing page 32)* and "weed holders."

Each strip requires a thirty-six-end warp. The projects were planned to encourage the reader to put on six different warps. Remember, the more often the process is repeated the more adept the weaver becomes at it and the more basic it all seems.

If you're ambitious enough to want to make pillows, placemats, or small rugs, just put on wider and, if necessary, longer warps, following the same warping pattern and weaving instructions. A three-hundred-sixty-end warp is only 10 × 36.

Before you begin to make a warp you should calculate the amount of yarn or thread that will be necessary to complete it. There's nothing more frustrating than running out in the middle, especially when using a material that is not readily available.

The calculations are very easy to make. Multiply the number of ends per inch (epi) by the width then the length. Shrinkage and **loom waste** also play a part, but, as will be seen in a moment, they are not difficult to calculate.

The warps in the first strip exercises are made of a 3/2 perle cotton. Any thread of the same or similar size may be substituted. There is only one rule to remember here: the epi is governed by the weight of the thread or yarn. The heavier it is, the fewer epi are used; for lighter materials, more are used (*i.e.,* for a 5/2 perle, try 15 epi). The reason for this is obvious. It takes more ends per inch to make a firm fabric with lighter weight yarn.

A pound of 3/2 perle cotton thread has 1,260 yards in it. Chapter Two explained how to find out how many yards there are in a pound of cotton.

Each of the six strips will be worked on only eighteen inches of warp, but extra length must be added to the total to account for **loom waste.** Loom waste (see **thrum** in the warping glossary) is the amount of material needed to tie the warp onto the cloth and warp beams and to reach from the warp beam through the heddles and reed to where the actual weaving will be done.

The amount of loom wastage depends upon the size and type of loom that is used. There is about half a yard of wastage on a table loom and one to one and one half on a large floor loom. A three-yard warp will be more than sufficient for all looms and will allow for samples as well as additional small projects in the case of some of the looms.

In planning the width of a fabric, ten percent should be added to the calculations for the warp, for shrinkage. A three-inch warp at twelve epi should have forty ends (12 × 3 plus 10%). For the total

yardage necessary, multiply this by three, and the result comes to 120 yards. 3/2 perle cotton is available in two-ounce spools. Each of these spools contains 157.5 yards (1,260 divided by 8). Twelve of these (two in each of the six colors used in the strips) will be more than enough for both the warps and all the weaving to be done in the entire project.

PREPARING THE LOOM FOR WARPING

Prepare your loom ahead of time so that you will not have to interrupt the process of putting a warp on it. First of all, the beater must be carrying a reed with a sufficient number of dents to handle the epi. In the case of a reed with fewer dents per inch than the epi called for in the project, some of the threads must be doubled up. With a larger number of dents than epi, some must be skipped. For example, every fourth dent must be skipped when threading twelve epi on a fifteen-dent reed.

The following chart will help when a reed with the proper number of dents is not available.

8-dent reed
10 epi: two ends in every fourth dent per inch.
12 epi: two ends in every other dent per inch.
15 epi: two ends in each dent except the first per inch.
10-dent reed
8 epi: skip every fourth dent per inch.
12 epi: two ends in every fifth dent per inch.
15 epi: two ends in every other dent per inch.
12-dent reed
8 epi: skip every third dent per inch.
10 epi: skip every sixth dent per inch.
15 epi: two ends in every fourth dent per inch.
15-dent reed
8 epi: skip one dent after each dent threaded except after the eighth of every inch.
10 epi: skip every third dent per inch.
12 epi: skip every fourth dent per inch.

Before warping, the weaver should also be certain that there are sufficient heddles on each harness. (*See photograph 35 on page 40*).

One of the most worthwhile investments in weaving equipment is a good **warping board** or **reel** (*see photograph 40*). If for some reason the weaver does not have one, there are ways of improvising. There's no reason to be leery about using a little ingenuity. After all, warps are still being made on stakes in the ground in many parts of the world that are justly famous for the fine quality of their woven products. The only important constant is putting in the cross to keep the warp ends in order for threading on the loom.

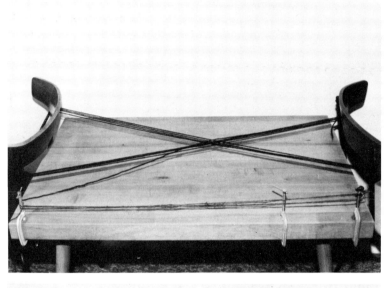

37 A warping board improvised of two chairs at opposite ends of a small table. The cross is in the middle.

38 Another board is made of C clamps attached upside down along the edges of a thirty-six-inch table. If the table is valued, it's a good idea to pad the wood with cloth to protect the surface. In this case, the cross is in the lower right-hand corner between the two sets of tied dark string.

39 For short narrow warps, small Tinker Toy sets can be used. The cross is in the upper right corner between the sets of light string.

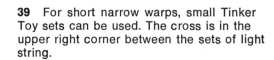

40 In this set of illustrations, a three-yard warp 36 ends wide is being wound on a warping board. A single spool of thread is used. To do this, a guide string was made of a ten-yard piece of cord, knotted at every yard, to see which pegs were to be used. The cord is knotted on the top right peg, goes under the second, over the third, around the fourth down to the right peg on the second row, around it, over to the left second row, up around it, and back. These two rows proved correct, and the warp thread is put on following the same path as the cord. After this the guide is removed.

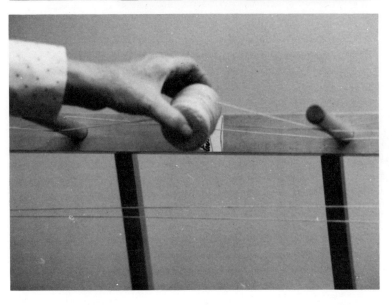

41 Now make the cross: going from right to left, it's under the second peg and over the third. Completing the circuit by coming from left back to right, it's the reverse: around peg four on left, under peg three, over peg two, and back around peg one to start over again.

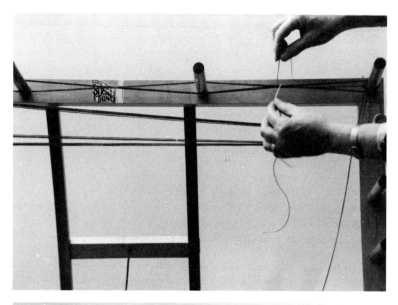

42 To keep track of the number of ends wound, loop a piece of string around every ten lengths. For this three-yard (12 epi) warp, the fourth loop will mark the finish.

43 If a knot appears in the spool or if it is necessary to attach another piece of thread to complete the warping, go back to the first or last peg, cut out knot and retie there, or knot on new thread there.

44 A miswound thread at the cross.

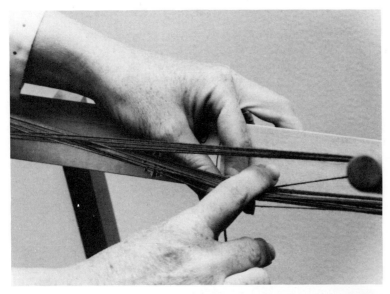

45 To correct the miswound thread, pull it to its proper place with your fingers.

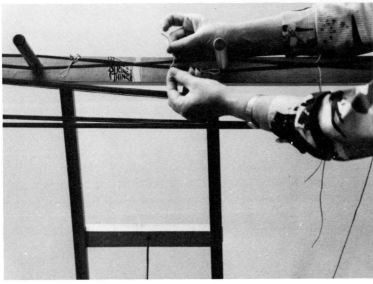

46 After completing the proper number of ends, tie pieces of string around each of the four bars of the cross.

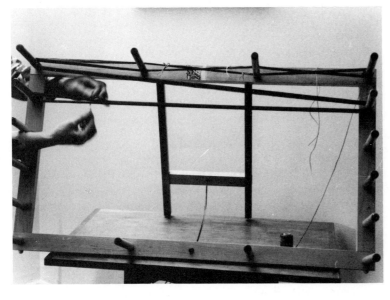

47 Tie a string, binding the end of the warp into a loop near the last peg.

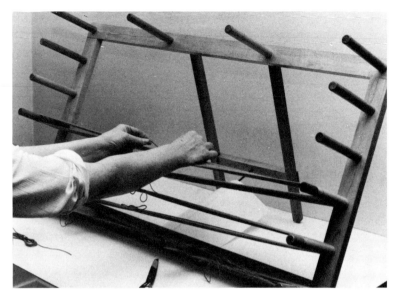

48 Sometimes it's more comfortable to warp from a sitting position using the bottom pegs instead of the top ones. The procedure is exactly the same except that one mounts rows of pegs instead of descending them.

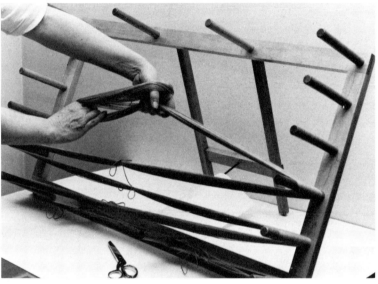

49 Chain the warp by removing it from the last peg and putting your hand through the loop created there and pulling up another loop through it. Continue making these loops and pulling them through each other until you approach the cross. Tie the last loop to the warp to prevent unraveling.

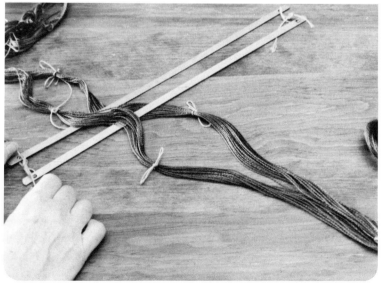

50 Remove the warp from the board and insert lease sticks (flat sticks with holes at the ends available at all suppliers). The lease sticks are placed at either side of the intersection of the cross. Tie them with strings at the end to prevent them from falling out.

Dressing the Loom

The first method to be described is the easiest for a novice working alone. It involves threading the warp from the front through the reed and heddles to the warp beam.

51 Tie the lease sticks containing the warp to the front or breast beam of the loom with the short end and cross of the warp facing the reed.

52 Tie the beater to the front beam by putting cord through one of the dents of the reed and looping around it and the beam. Choose a dent sufficiently near the end of the reed so that it will not be used for "denting the warp" (threading the warp through the reed). This tie will hold the reed upright for the denting.

53 Untie the strings that were used to hold the warp in place. Also get rid of any bits of string in the chain used to count ends in warping. Untie the string, holding the last loop of the chain to the warp.

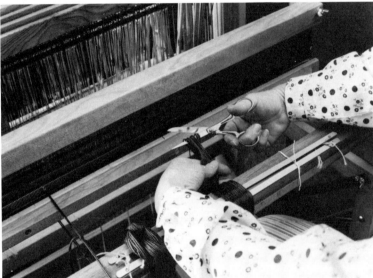

54 Cut the loops at end of the warp beyond the cross.

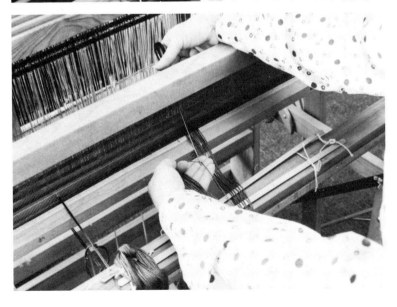

55 Center 36 ends of warp with lease sticks attached to the front beam. Find the center dent of the reed. With a sleying hook, start sleying (threading) the warp ends through the reed. Begin 18 dents from the center dent with the first end. The purpose of the cross is now evident. The warp ends go alternately under and over the lease sticks, keeping them in order.

56 Spools of yarn can be placed under the harnesses to lift them to a comfortable height for threading. Either with a threading hook or by hand, thread the warp through the heddles, following the draft (see illustrations 8 and 9 facing page 64.)

57 Check units of threading after every set of four ends to make certain that you have made no mistakes. Continue across the warp until all ends have been threaded.

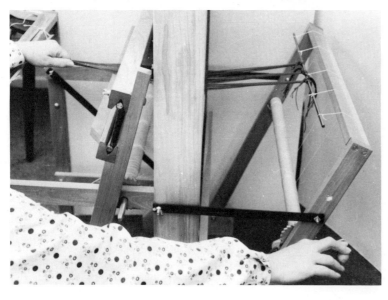

58 Start winding the warp onto the warp beam. Hold the warp in firm grasp pulling it taut in front of the loom, in order to wind the warp on under tension.

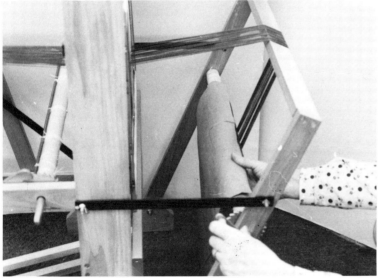

59 If the loom is too big to hold the warp while winding, weight it with a book on the floor in front of the loom.

60 When the rod actually reaches the warp beam, start winding heavy paper with the warp. The paper should be wider than the warp to prevent the ends from slipping off. The paper will keep all warp ends at an even tension. Without the paper, some threads would slip into previous layers while others would pile up on each other.

65 Cut the string, holding the beater in place. Remove the cord, holding the chain up, and unchain enough warp to reach the floor in front of the loom.

62 Keep winding the warp on the warp beam until the front and free end of the warp reaches the front beam. Bring up the tie rod of the cloth beam and tie the warp on in bouts. (See photographs 58 to 60 on pages 50-51.)

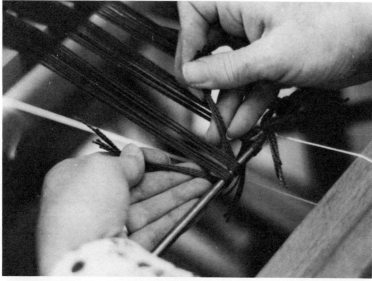

63 In bouts (one-inch sections), tie the warp to the cloth-beam tie-on rod. Be certain that the apron or cords come up over the back beam.

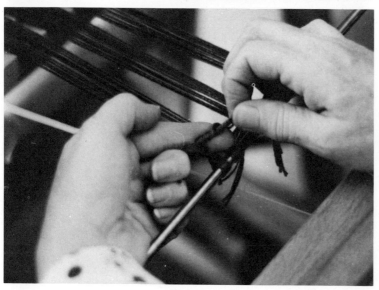

64 Bring divided sections over the bout and twist the right half around the left half *twice*.

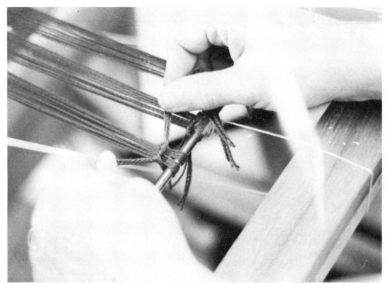

65 Tighten by pulling on the ends.

66 Check that the tension is even by pressing down on each bout.

67 If necessary, adjust the tension by pulling two tie ends in opposite directions until the desired tension is achieved.

68 Weave in a few rows of rag strips or thrums. Now the project is ready for weaving.

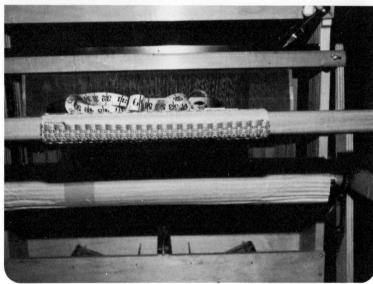

69 After several inches of weaving—and where after adjusting the brakes, the warp is advanced to the point of contact of tie-on knots with cloth beams—cover them with a strip of corrugated paper (or other heavy paper) to keep the knots from wrinkling the newly woven cloth.

Preparing the Shuttles

Now that the loom is warped, the only thing that remains to be done is to prepare the weft or filling material by mounting it in a shuttle.

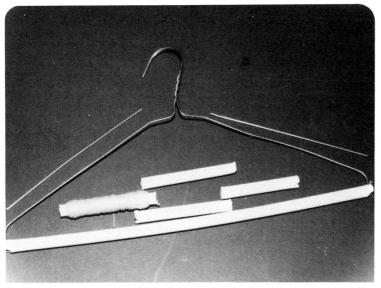

70 If commercial bobbins for boat shuttles are unavailable, they can be made by cutting the cardboard tubing from a cleaner's hanger to size. The wire can be cut and used to mount small hangings.

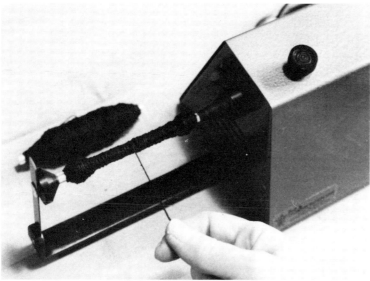
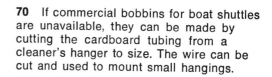

71 When putting thread, yarn, or fiber on these improvised bobbins, "hill up" at the ends first, then evenly guide the filling material back and forth across the bobbin.

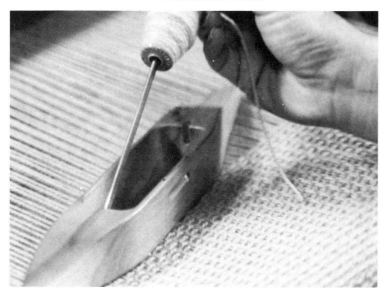

72 With a plastic bobbin, insert on boat shuttle pin with large hole toward hinge. (The smaller hole at the opposite end can get caught on the hinge stopping the free flow of weft material.)

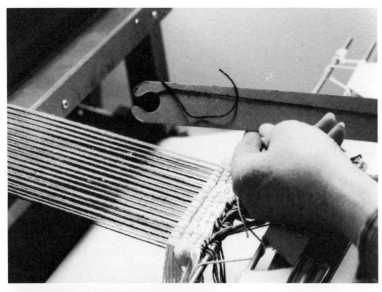

73 To wind the stick or ski shuttle, start by tying the end of the filling material to the shuttle with a slip knot to keep the filling material from completely unraveling.

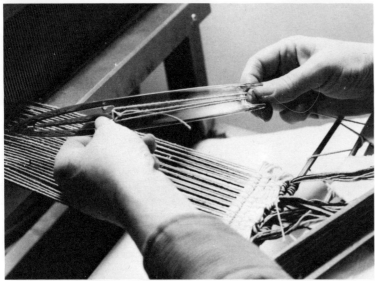

74 To wind a netting shuttle (excellent for samples and small warps like this three-inch one), knot the weft material to the center post, bring strand to the bottom of the shuttle, and turn shuttle over.

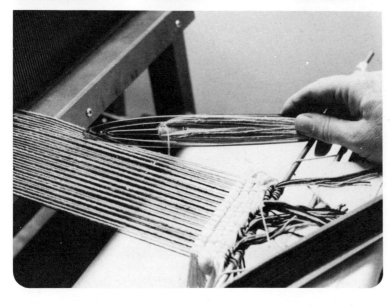

75 Bring the yarn back up around the center post then down again, and turn the shuttle over. Repeat until desired amount of material is wound.

Using Two or More Shuttles

Two or more shuttles are used when the pattern requires two or more different colors or textures in the filling material.

76 When working with more than one shuttle, arrange them with the one to be used first nearest the beater and the one to be used last nearest the weaver. After a shuttle is used, place it behind the others. Always use the shuttle at the top for the next row. This will keep them in order in all cases except when more than one pick (weft row) of the same material is used in succession. In that case, some care must be taken at the start but, after a while, a natural work rhythm will evolve.

77 Interlock the weft threads or yarns at the selvedges, except when two separate layers are being woven. (This will be explained later in Chapter 5.)

Making a Butterfly

A **butterfly** is used instead of a shuttle to carry filling through the warp shed. It is light and flexible and can be used for narrow warps and in patterns that call for weft shots that only extend a fraction of the way across the warp.

78 To make a butterfly, wind material around thumb and little finger in a figure eight.

79 Push the end of the yarn under the yarn at your palm. Enough should be put through to circle the butterfly.

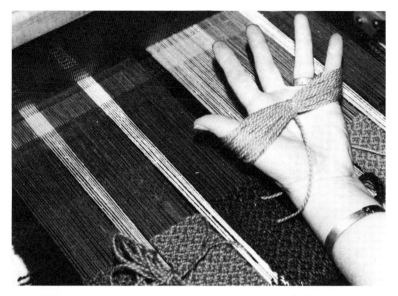

80 Complete by wrapping two or three loops around the center of the butterfly.

81 The thread or yarn feeds from the untied end of the butterfly. Here it is used to find the center of a web. It is stretched the whole width, then folded in half.

82 Using the butterfly to make a weft inset through only a part of the warp.

Handy Hints

83 To correct a broken warp end, cut a length of same material sufficient to finish the weaving. Remove the broken warp end from the heddle and reed, and thread in the new length. Pin it to the web at the point where the end is broken.

84 Weight the other end of new thread (washers or a fishing weight will do) and hang it over the back beam. Continue to weave as before. Be careful to let out lengths of the new thread in same amount as warp released for working.

85 To change the threading of the warp on the loom without removing it, open the two tabby sheds and insert lease sticks near the back beam to preserve the cross. Tie the sticks to the beam. Cut the warp in front of the reed and pull back, removing it from the heddles and dents. Take the old web off the cloth beam. Rethread from back to front. Go through heddles first, in order of new draft, then through the dents, and finally tie to cloth beam rod.

86 When weaving in strips of cloth, overlap ends and beat hard.

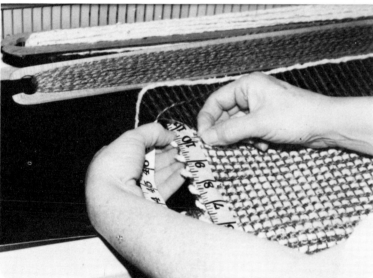

87 Pin a tape measure to the selvedge to keep track of length woven.

Glossary of Weaving Equipment

88 RUG BEATER Used when extra firmness of beat is needed as in rug weaving.

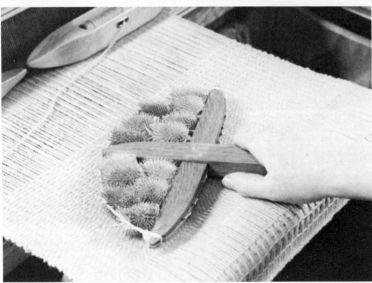

89 TEASEL Used to raise the nap on woolen cloth.

90 TEMPLE or STRETCHER Wood or metal implement adjustable in width, with nails at both ends, extending to the selvedge, and used to maintain even width of fabric while weaving.

5 THE STRIPS

The six strips *(see color photograph 1 facing page 32)* and the small hangings *(see color photograph 2 facing page 32)* have been designed to introduce the new weaver to the craft. They show some of the possibilities for weaving on two- and four-harness looms. The two-harness weaves can also be woven on the rigid-heddle loom (see Appendix) or on any other simple shedding weaving device.

In these charming strips, which are only three by eighteen inches; over forty-eight weaving and warping techniques are used. Why not follow along and do them with us? By the time you've finished, you'll find that you have mastered enough patterns and variations to do endless projects of your own. What you weave will simply be a matter of the dimensions of the warp you use, and that's only a question of repetition of the basic procedures.

The entire warp of each strip is made of a different color. In order of use, the colors are violet, blue, green, yellow, orange, and red. The weaving is done in the same color for background (*i.e.,* strip 1 is violet on violet) and the next color on the wheel for accent (blue on violet). With strip 6, red, we return to strip 1's violet for the accents.

These are all "safe" color combinations, but there's enough warp on the loom to do all manner of experimentation both with the colors and the textures of weft threads. Why not try an orange weft yarn on the violet warp thread just to see what happens? It might suggest a smashing pillow project.

It has already been mentioned that two two-ounce 3/2 perle cotton spools of each color will be sufficient for completing all six strips (and then some). On projects involving other threads, yarns, or fibers, you'll probably want to figure out how much yardage is necessary before beginning. You already know how to find the total for warp (*see page 42*). For weft, the best thing is to make a sample. You can go right back to the good old index card. (See photographs 17 and 18 on page 28.)

Warp what's necessary for the warp, then thread a needle with the weft material and weave for one inch. Count the number of picks. Multiply that by the length of warp to be used and then by the width.

Let's suppose there are ten weft picks per inch of 3/2 perle cotton for the three-by-eighteen-inch

STRIP 1

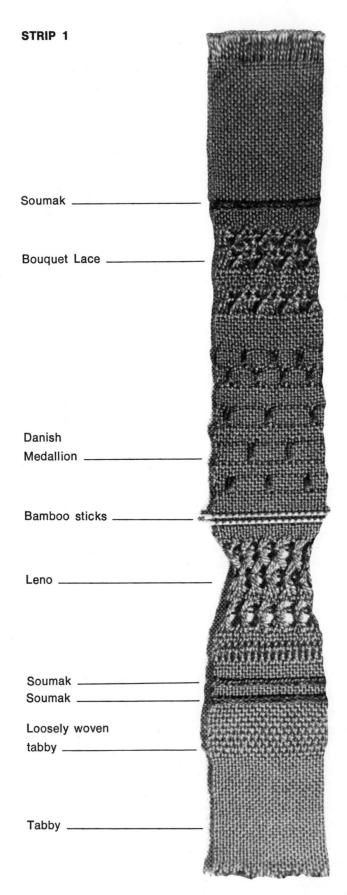

Soumak ——————————————

Bouquet Lace ——————————

Danish
Medallion ———————————————

Bamboo sticks ——————————

Leno ————————————————

Soumak ————————————————
Soumak ————————————————

Loosely woven
tabby ——————————————————

Tabby ——————————————————

strip. Your first multiplication is 10 × 18; or the number of weft picks per inch times the length of the strip. That gives you 180. Your next multiplication is 180 × 3⅓. The 3 represents the three-inch width of the strip and the ⅓ represents the ten percent shrinkage allowance. The total is 600. That total is in inches and must be divided by 36 to find the yardage, which is 16⅔ yards (be a sport and buy seventeen).

If it takes 120 yards to make each warp for the strips and seventeen yards for the wefts, it is apparent that one two-ounce spools in each color (157.5 yards) would be sufficient for all six, if you were doing the project and nothing else. We suggest two spools so that you can have fun. There's enough warp to experiment with making samples, hangings, weed holders, and other things. Why not do it? We promise you'll have a marvelous time following your own creative impulses.

Commercially made luggage racks are available in every department store. By taking off their strips and putting on yours, you'll have a lovely addition to any guest room *(see color photograph 1 facing page 32)*. If you don't need another luggage rack for guests, make one for yourself. It's the perfect height to use as a table next to the loom to hold the mountain of paraphernalia that weavers do accumulate as they ply their craft. The rack is also a good size and height to hold a table loom. On it, the loom is low enough so that you don't have to stretch to reach the levers.

Let's start weaving.

STRIP 1

Warp: 3/2 perle cotton, violet
Weft: same as warp plus 3/2 perle cotton, blue
Reed: 12 dents per inch *(or see table on page 42)*
Sett (number of warp threads): 12 epi
Width: 3 inches (approx.)

9 Pillow made on same warp as the seven-thread yarn stole. Seven novelty yarns woven in as one. Plain weaves throughout.

8 Shawl woven on a spaced warp threaded with yarn made up of seven different strands. Plain weave with leno border.

10 Another pillow on same spaced warp with multiple ends of brown yarn stripes.

12 Twill samplers. Red, white, and blue rug yarn on 8/4 cotton warp.

11 Placemats done with red and blue rag strip wefts on log cabin warp threading.

13 and 14 Fronts and backs of three pillows woven on rosepath threading.

15 A shower of pillows that are all easy to weave using instructions in this book.

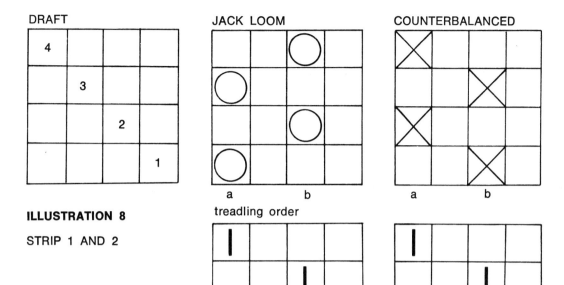

DRAFT

4			
	3		
		2	
			1

ILLUSTRATION 8

STRIP 1 AND 2

JACK LOOM

treadling order

COUNTERBALANCED

a   b

a   b

Tabby

Illustration 8 shows the draft, tie-up, and treadling order for both Jack and counter-balanced looms. It is for the **tabby** or plain weave (which is the interplacement of one warp thread and one weft thread alternately across the entire width). Variations on this basic weave are infinite and offer endless challenging possibilities.

Table looms use the same instructions as the Jack loom. Depress levers 1 and 3 for the *a* shed and 2 and 4 for the *b* shed.

ILLUSTRATION 9

STRIP 1 AND 2

2	
	1

Illustration 9 is the draft for a two-harness loom.

On rigid-heddle looms, the threads passing through the slots can represent *a* shed and those through the eyes *b* shed.

Make a warp according to instructions in Chapter 4, and dress the loom following the drafts in the above illustrations.

91 After loading the shuttle with thread, start weaving by stepping on treadle "a" and opening the first tabby shed. "Throw" the shuttle through from left to right. Leave a tail of about two inches of weft at the left selvedge.

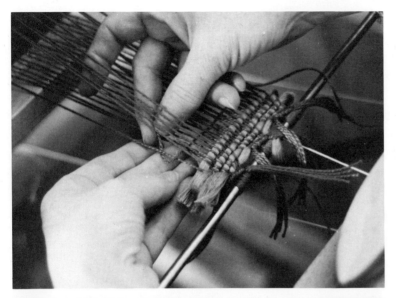

92 Fold the weft tail around the first warp thread and back into the still open shed.

93 Release the harnesses and close the shed. With the beater, gently "beat" the first weft pick into place against the rag strips.

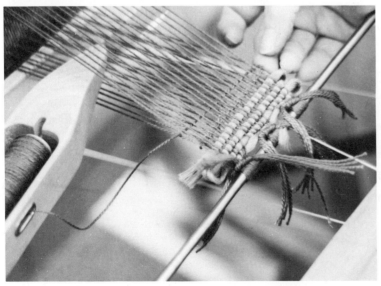

94 Change sheds (step on "b" treadle). Turn the weft around the right selvedge (first right warp thread) without leaving a weft loop or pulling in the warp. Throw the shuttle. The weft should always lay at an angle in the shed. Close the harness and gently beat the weft. Try to maintain an even beat. The space between the weft shots should be the same as between the warp ends. Continue weaving.

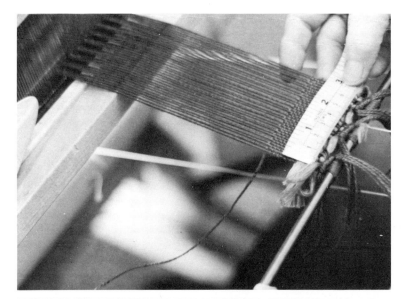

95 After about an inch, check the width of the web. Try to maintain an even width for the entire length of the project. This means you must pay constant attention to the selvedges. Continue plain weave for about 3½ inches.

96 For a looser, more open fabric, beat still more gently to leave more space between the weft shots.

Soumak

Soumak is an embellishing weave that is used to give added texture to fabric. The technique is also used to weave entire rugs. It is similar to the stem stitch in embroidery and often used for the same purpose of outlining specific design and pattern motifs. Soumak can be done with either a butterfly or shuttle. Open the shed for the next tabby shot. Place the tail of the new soumak thread from the left selvedge, extending in about four warp ends. Close the shed. Beat gently. *Do not open the shed again.* Soumak is done with the shed closed.

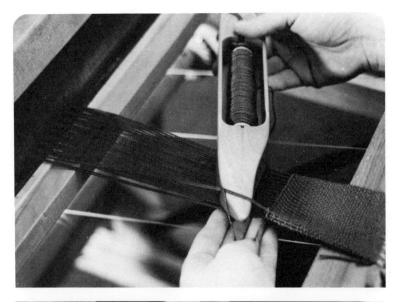

97 From the left selvedge, pass the blue weft end over the first four warp ends, then back under two. Go over the next four and back under two, and continue this wrapping action across the entire row.

98 Alternate tabby rows between soumak rows. If the edge warp end is not raised, catch it with the shuttle to keep the selvedge even.

99 Pass the shuttle back to the left side.

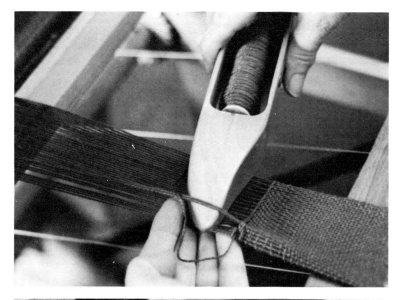

100 Do another row of soumak.

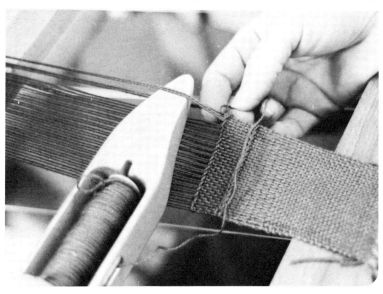

101 Tabby shots may be eliminated. Catch the edge of the warp to the right.

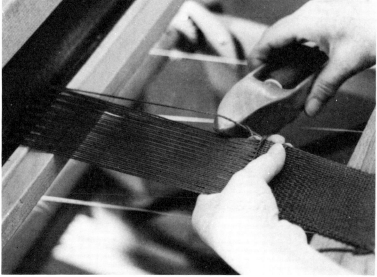

102 Reverse direction of soumak.

Leno

Leno is one of the lace weaves. It is used for borders as well as for overall effects. *The shed is again closed and the warp flat.*

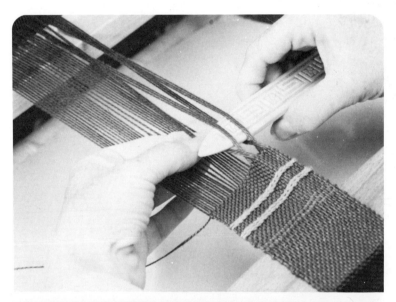

103 With your hand, pick up the first three warp ends on the right. Using a pick-up stick (or any broad flat stick with a point), pick up the next three warp ends (fourth, fifth, and sixth). Bring the first three ends to the left over the second three, twisting them around and under the pick-up stick. Repeat this three by three across the row.

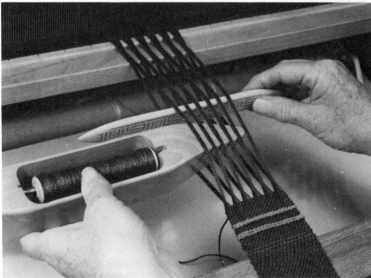

104 Make a shed by turning the pick-up stick on its side, and pass the shuttle through it. Always use the pick-up stick to hold the warp twist.

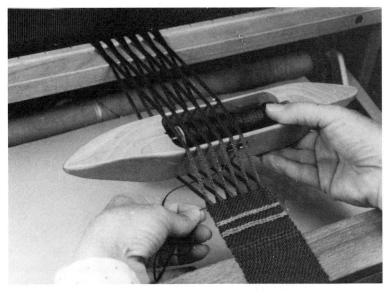

105 Hold the weft end at the left selvedge to maintain the width of the fabric.

106 Three ends were used for the above to keep an even number of twists across the row. *Any number of ends can be twisted.* They can even vary from row to row (*i.e.,* two over two, then three over three on next row; you can even twist only the center warps). Always use the pick-up stick to twist the weft into place.

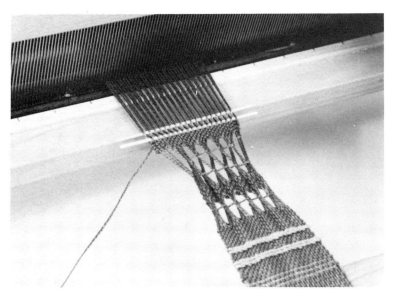

107 When weaving narrow strips, it's sometimes difficult to regain your original width. Bamboo skewers can be cut and inserted in the next two tabby sheds to spread out the fabric.

Danish Medallion

Danish medallion is another embellishing weave. It is especially popular in the Scandinavian countries and is used for borders and overall decorative effects. It is a weft design in that it is made completely by weft ends. Use the blue thread (or any contrasting color to the warp) wound on a flat shuttle or into a butterfly.

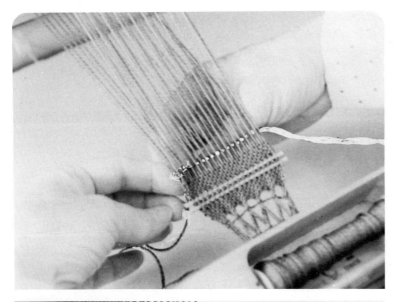

108 Open the next tabby shed. Pass the pattern thread through it, tucking the tail back into the same shed. Close and beat gently.

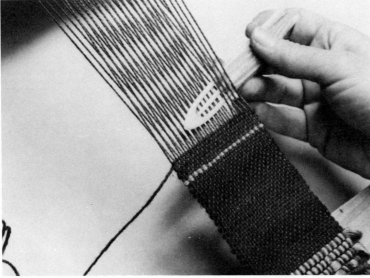

109 Weave an odd number of tabby rows (about ½ inch). In the next shed, pass the shuttle or butterfly carrying the pattern weft through to the point where first medallion is desired (in this photograph, this is after the fourth warp end) and bring it up through the warp. Do not close the shed again.

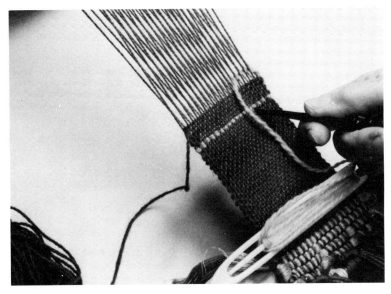

110 Insert a crochet needle through the web under the first pattern shot, and on the same warp line you came through on with the second weft shot.

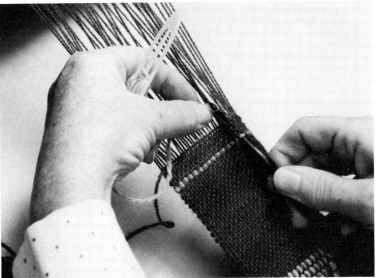

111 Catch the second pattern shot with the hook of the needle. Pull a loop down under the web and back up to the surface at the point where the needle was originally inserted.

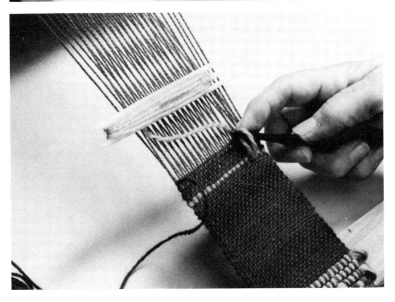

112 Bring the loop up to the second pattern line.

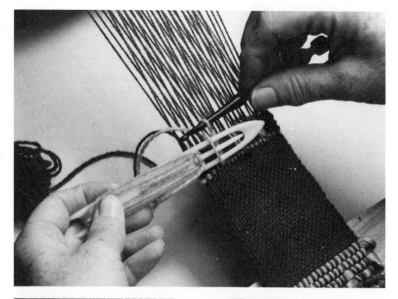

113 Holding the loop open with the needle, insert the shuttle or butterfly carrying pattern thread back through the loop. (We used a picture of a later medallion for clarity.)

114 Pull the pattern thread to adjust the size of the medallion.

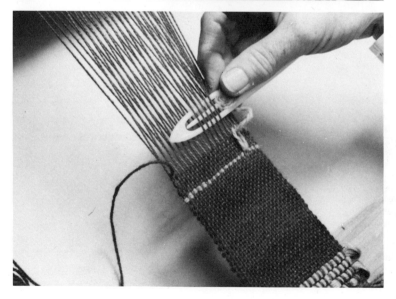

115 Replace the shuttle or butterfly into the shed and bring it up again at the point where the second medallion is desired. Repeat steps 110 through 115. Continue in this manner for as many medallions as may be desired in the row.

116 Medallion loops may either be left flat or pulled up tight depending on taste or the effect desired. To finish, cut weft pattern thread, leaving a small tail. Fold the tail back into the shed, close, and beat.

Bouquet Lace

Bouquet lace is frequently called Brooks bouquet in honor of Marguerite Brooks who made it so popular with contemporary weavers. It is the easiest of the lace weaves because, among other things, it requires no pick-up stick.

117 Weave about one inch of tabby. End at a row where the shuttle is on the right. Open the tabby shed which has the right selvedge thread down, cut the weft thread, and start again (with tail insert) at the right to have the shuttle and shed in the correct positions. Pass the shuttle under the first four raised warp ends on the right.

118 Bring the shuttle back over the four weft ends and pass under the first eight weft ends. Bring shuttle out.

119 Hold the right end of the web and pull the weft thread to tighten the loop. Loop around again over four warp ends (the fourth to eighth) and come out again after eight (actually the twelfth warp end).

120 Continue to the end of the row, under eight and back over four. Weave an odd number of tabby rows so that the shuttle is again at the right for another bouquet row. Catch the weft around the right-selvedge warp end to maintain even width.

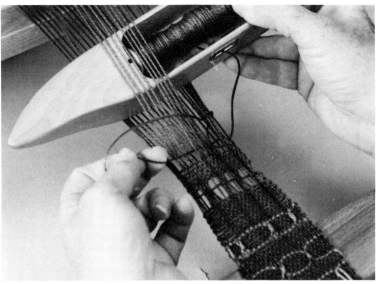

121 Begin second row exactly as first was begun.

122 Continue under eight over four until the end of the second row of bouquet lace. Finish the strip with two more rows of soumak and three inches of tabby.

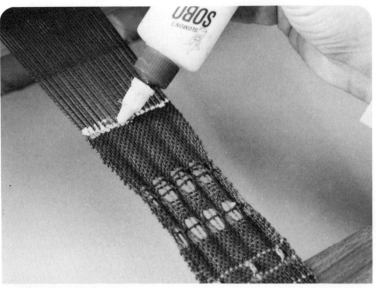

Finishing

123 After the weaving is completed, apply white glue to the last row.

124 Spread it evenly with your finger and remove excess.

Laid In _____

Slits _____

Spanish
Lace _____

Loops _____

Clasped Weft _____

Tabby alternating
wefts _____

Tabby contrasting
weft _____

Tabby warp and weft
same color _____

STRIP 2

Warp: 3/2 perle cotton, blue
Weft: 3/2 perle cotton, blue and green
Reed: 12 dent
Sett: 1 per cent (12 epi)
Width: 3 inches (approx.)

(See Illustrations 8 and 9 on page 65 for draft, tie-up, and treadling order.)

This strip will explore more variations of the tabby or plain weave that can be done on any two-harness loom as well as on four or more. There will be particular emphasis on color and the variety of effects that can be worked by only adding one additional weft shade to a pattern. (See photographs 125 through 138 on pages 80-85.)

After trying out the technique illustrated in this strip, it's time you did a little exploring. On the warp that remains after you complete Strip 2, combine the colors in a manner that is pleasing with the techniques in Strip 1. Use more than two colors in the weft and see what happens. The result might be more dazzling than anything shown in this book —and more exciting, because it's yours and yours alone.

Let yourself go. Try whatever catches your fancy. Threads of other weights, yarns, fibers, anything that happens to be in the work basket. Now that you're really weaving, your reward should be the joy of savoring the endless combinations, the marvelous possibilities that are only just beginning to occur to you.

125 Weave three inches of tabby with blue weft. When starting a new length of weft yarn of the same or a different color, open the next shed, fold the end of the old weft into it, and have the new weft overlap it. Close the shed and beat.

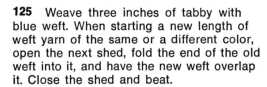

126 At the bottom is tabby with the same color weft as warp.

Above it, tabby with a different same-color weft (in this case, green on a blue warp). Above that, tabby is done with two shuttles, one filled with green and the other with blue. They are laid in alternately. (See photographs 76 and 77 on page 57.)

Above that, **clasped weft.** To do it, start with one shuttle at each selvedge (green at right, blue at left). Open the shed. Bring the right shuttle through the shed and loop its thread around the left weft. Then bring the shuttle back through the shed to the right side.

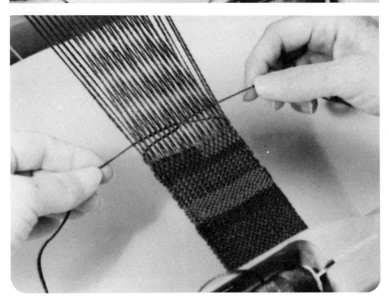

127 Pull the right thread, bringing its clasped left thread with it, until both are positioned where you want them. Close the shed and beat. These clasped positions can float in the web simply by pulling the ends in succeeding sheds and sliding the clasp to the right or left. Continue for ½ inch, then reverse the shuttle so green is on the left and blue on the right and continue for another ½ inch.

Loops

Simple **loops** often appear in the weaving of Greece, Portugal, Spain, Italy, Central America, and Quebec (where the technique is called "boutonné"). They add design to a simple tabby background. The loops may be of the same color and thread as the background or of another strand and color for special effects. Simple geometric designs are best for looping, and they can be worked out in advance on graph paper.

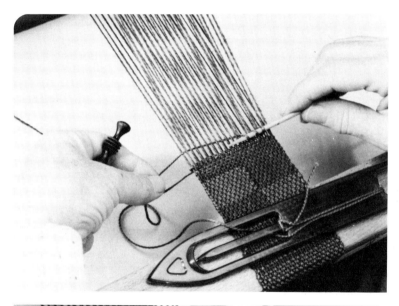

128 Do a few rows of blue-on-blue tabby. Open the next shed, and lay in a green weft shot. With the shed still open, pull up loops of it onto a double-ended knitting needle or pointed skewer. (A crochet hook may be used to place the loops.)

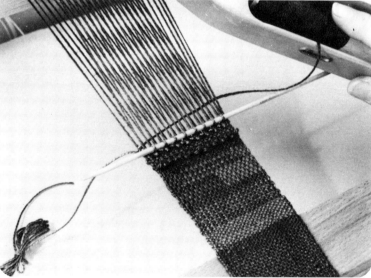

129 Change sheds and weave a blue tabby shot. After closing this shed and beating, remove the needle. Repeat for length of design. *Remember, a tabby shot follows each row of loops.*

Spanish Lace

Spanish lace is named for its use in linen weaving
in Spain. It is woven by having the weft wander
back and forth traveling from selvedge to selvedge.
Because it is too time-consuming to be practical in
an overall design, it is usually reserved for borders.

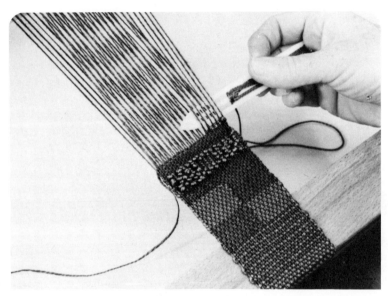

130 Here, the weft is green, but it might
be the same color as the warp. Open the
shed, with shuttle on the right, and pass it
left under the first six raised warp ends.

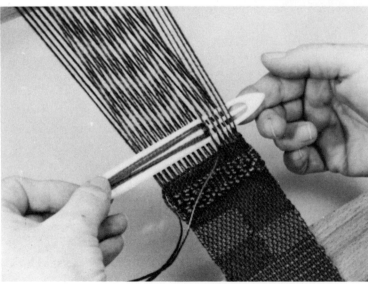

131 Open the next shed, return the
shuttle from the left to the right under the
six warp ends.

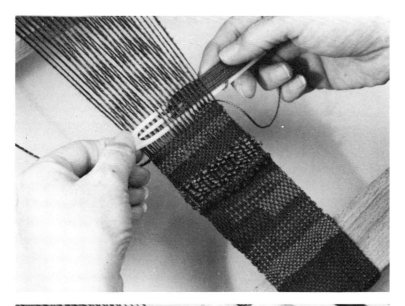

132 Change sheds. Weave right to left under twelve warp ends.
Repeat back and fourth weaving all the way across the row.

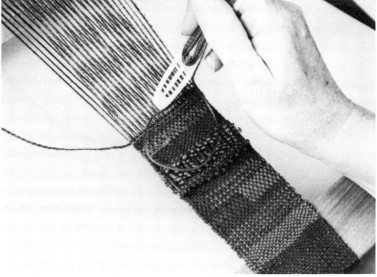

133 Use the shuttle to ease the pattern into place. *Do not beat.* Beating may distort the effect you are trying to create.

134 The number of warp ends the weft passes back and forth under may vary. They can even occur in the middle of rows. The number of lace rows may also vary as may the tabby rows between them.

In Strip 3 there are three bands of Spanish lace between tabby bands.

Slits

Slits are useful for emphasizing designs, holding drawstrings, making buttonholes, and for all those purposes for which a vertical opening might be desired.

Because the weft shots will not be going from selvedge to selvedge, a separate shuttle or butterfly is needed for each of the areas from selvedge to first slit, from slit to slit, and from last slit to the other selvedge.

135 With three butterflies, weave back and forth in the three sections. Open the shed, lay in the first butterfly from the selvedge to the first slit and bring it out. Lay in the second butterfly from the first to the second slit and bring it out. Lay in the third butterfly from the second slit to the other selvedge. Close the shed and beat. Open the next shed and repeat. Continue for desired length of slit (about one inch). To close the slits, weave across the entire row with one of the butterflies coming from a selvedge. Cut off the other two butterflies. When closing row is completed and beaten, if that butterfly is not wanted for additional weaving, cut it off.

Laid in

There are many ways in which pattern thread or yarn can be added to the weave to create a design. The most basic way is to **lay in** a pattern thread in the same shed as a tabby shot. In these cases the designs may be plotted on graph paper first. The weaving is usually done on the reverse side of the fabric. When the fabric is removed from the loom and is turned right side up, it hides the loop formed by carrying the pattern thread from one section to another in the design.

Working with a simple geometric shape such as a square or a monogram, the pattern can be laid in on the top surface. The pattern material should be heavier or of a different color than the tabby weft (in this case green with blue).

136 Open the shed and lay in butterflies where design is desired, folding ends into shed. Close shed. Beat into place. It is sometimes easier to push the pattern into place with your finger.

137 Follow with tabby shot in *same* shed. Change sheds. Repeat. *All beating must be very easy in order to prevent distortion in the plain weave around the design.*

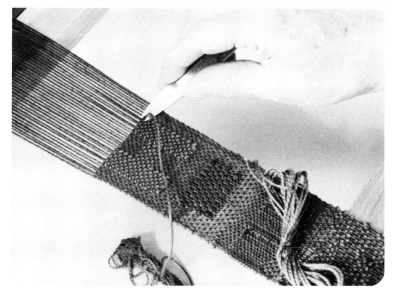

138 For the bar in "H," one of the butterflies is laid in straight across. Be sure you end the last shot at the original side. After finishing design with tabby shot, clip off pattern threads. Block letters are good practice design units.

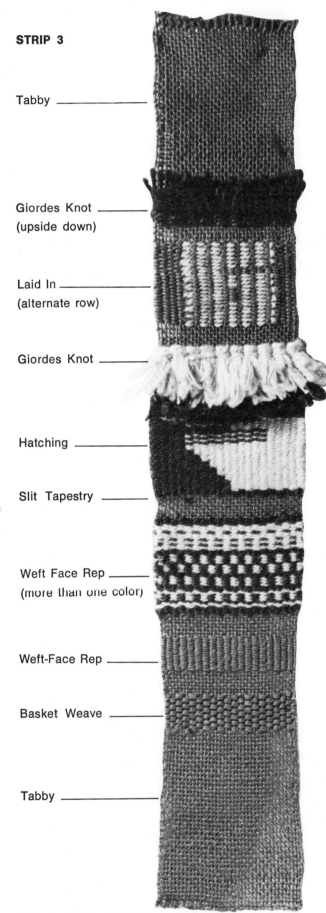

Tabby _____

Giordes Knot _____
(upside down)

Laid In _____
(alternate row)

Giordes Knot _____

Hatching _____

Slit Tapestry _____

Weft Face Rep _____
(more than one color)

Weft-Face Rep _____

Basket Weave _____

Tabby _____

STRIP 3

Warp: 3/2 perle cotton (or 8/4 cotton rug warp),
   green
Weft: same as warp, plus 3/2 perle cotton, yellow;
   some wool rya yarn, green and yellow
Reed: 12 dent
Sett: 12 epi
Width: 3 inches (approx.)

ILLUSTRATION 10

STRIP 3

2 HARNESS DRAFT

2	2		
		1	1

a

tie-up

4 HARNESS DRAFT

4			
	3		
		2	
			1

b

JACK LOOM   tie-up

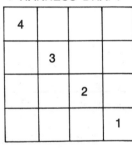
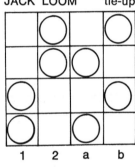

1   2   a   b

Illustration 10 indicates that there is a change in threading when Strip 3 is done on a two-harness loom. With the four-harness loom the threading remains as it was for the previous strips, but there is a change in the first and second tie-ups (the tabby treadles remain as before). The illustration is for a Jack loom. As you know, on a counter-balanced loom the tie-ups would be reversed.

On a rigid-heddle loom the first pair of warp ends would go through slots (threads 1 and 2), the second pair through eyes (3 and 4), the third pair through slots (5 and 6), the fourth pair through eyes (7 and 8), and so on all across the warp. Because you cannot move the threads close to each other, weaves like **basket weave** are very open on this type of loom.

Basket Weave

As is apparent from the drafts in Illustration 10 on page 86, basket weave is a plain weave with paired warp and weft threads. Two adjacents warp ends are lifted (or lowered) by each treadle.

On a two-harness loom, it is impossible to weave a true tabby with the basket weave threading, but on a four-harness loom it's only one more of the many weaves possible on a **straight threading.** (**Twill** and **straight draw** are synonymous terms.)

To start Strip 3:

Weave three inches of tabby (treadling with *a* and *b*). It will be a slightly different weave on a two-harness loom. Watch the fabric and try to keep it about the same texture as a tabby. Follow basket weave with ½ inch of tabby.

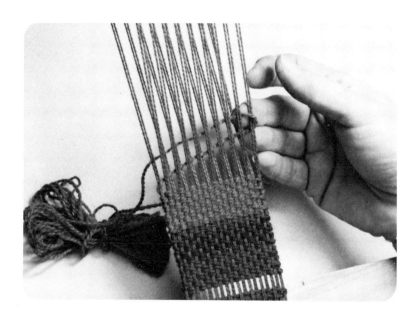

139 With the shed open, lay in a weft row of the same thread as was used to make the warp. *Do not close the shed.* Catch the weft around the selvedge thread (right or left depending on where you started) and lay in a second row in the same shed. Close the shed and beat very gently to keep the spacing of the weft the same as of the warp. *There will be two weft shots in each shed.* This can be done with a shuttle or a butterfly. Repeat for desired length (about ¾″).

Weft-Face Rep

Weft-face rep is a very effective pattern in which the beating is so hard that the warp completely disappears. Very interesting designs can be made by using two different colors of weft and alternating them in any manner you like (*see photograph 140 on following page*).

In Strip 3, ¾ inch of weft-face rep was woven with the same thread in weft and warp. This is ordinary weaving. Open treadle 1, lay in a weft pick, and then close it. *Beat very hard.*

Open treadle 2, lay in a pick, close, and beat so hard that the second weft shot slides into place next to the first, completely swallowing the warp so that it apparently disappears. When using more than one color, loop weft ends at selvedges for a firm edge.

For **Strip 3** do ½ inch of tabby between the weft-face rep, in the same color and thread for the weft and warp.

Vary the colors of the weft for 1½ inches. Use whatever design motif excites you.

Do ½ inch of tabby.

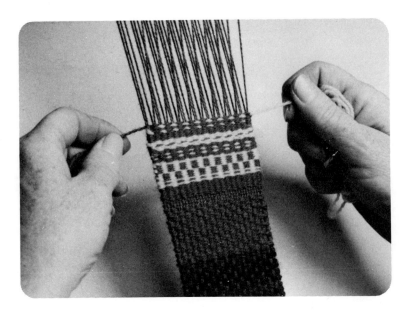

140 With two or more colors of weft, the variations of design possible in weft-face rep are almost inexhaustible.

Tapestry

Entire books have been written on **tapestry.** It is a very special category of weaving and over its long history many techniques have evolved that are special to it. The term *tapestry* generically refers to any piece of textile that hangs on the wall; modern pieces in which tapestry techniques may or may not be employed are sometimes called wall hangings.

Tapestry in its strictest sense refers to the very special Aubusson and Gobelin weft-faced weaves. The only difference between the two is the kind of loom on which they were woven: the Aubusson was developed in the Aubusson district of France and the Gobelin in the Paris workshops bearing that name. The weaves of the finished products look exactly the same.

True tapestry is woven with a separate shuttle, butterfly, or **tapestry bobbin** for each color and each section of design. Generally speaking, areas are woven one at a time and are not done row by row or from selvedge to selvedge.

Only a few very basic tapestry techniques will be discussed in this book. One of the most important things to bear in mind is that yarns or threads in adjacent areas are worked from the opposite directions. The reason for this will become clear as we go along.

Slit Tapestry

Slit tapestry gets its name from the fact that in this type of weave adjacent weft threads in the same rows do not intertwine; thus, tiny slits are formed where the two different threads meet. Usually they are of different colors but of the same measure or weight. Whole areas can be built up in one color before the next area is started.

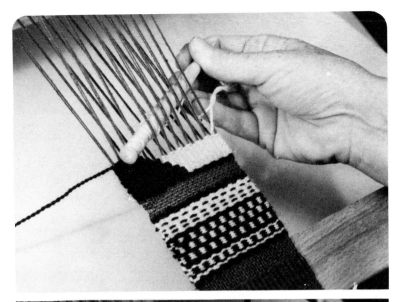

141 One inch of slit tapestry is used on Strip 3. Starting at the left, two rows of weft-face rep were done in the darker color bringing the tapestry bobbin (pictured here), butterfly, or shuttle back to the left. The entire dark area was then woven, gradually decreasing from half the width of the warp to one quarter of it. Starting at the right, the light area was filled in, with each weft shot coming right up to the dark thread but never overlapping or intertwining (as in clasped weft). Be careful that each row of light is in the same shed as the adjacent row of dark.

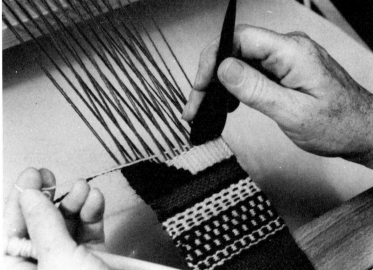

142 Obviously, the regular beater cannot be used for this weave. Beat each row with a tapestry beater (pictured here), a fork, or the tip of a tapestry bobbin.

Hatching

Hatching looks rather like clasped welt, but in hatching the welt threads never intertwine; they remain adjacent as in slit tapestry and consequently the color and thread blends are much smoother and more liquid. *(For instructions, see photographs 143 through 146 on pages 90-91.)*

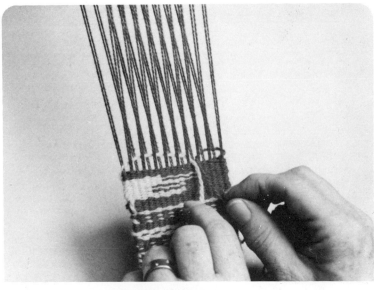

143 With wefts coming from opposite ends in the same shed, bring them to where you want the color to change. Lift them up through the warp. Close the shed.

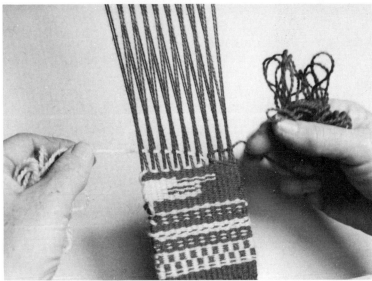

144 Change the shed and return the wefts to the selvedges. Be careful to catch the weft ends around the warp ends. Close the shed and beat.

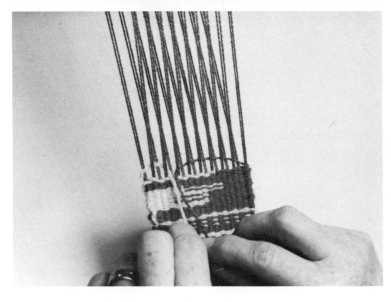

145 Repeat step 143 changing the placement of the colors.

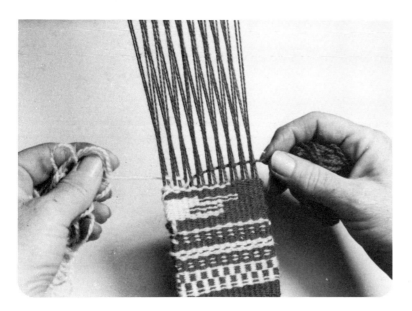

146 Repeat step 144. If you were to use two shades of the same color, a very subtle shading would be produced.

Wedge Shapes

Wedge shapes are another device for adding elements of color or texture to a design. The thread is held in a butterfly and before anything is done to the surrounding areas it is woven back and forth in the desired area, forming a wedge shape. A fork or tapestry beater does the beating.

147 After the wedge is woven in wedge shape, weave tabby in a contrasting thread across the entire width, easing the weft into place with a fork or tapestry beater. Build up each side of wedge *separately*, always easing the weft into place with a fork or beater, until the slides around the wedge are filled in and a weft shot can go from selvedge to selvedge in a straight line.

Giordes Knot

Technically speaking, **Giordes knot,** like all knots, comes under the classification of "wrapped wefts." Some Giordes knots can form "pile weaves." Whole rugs can be woven of rows of knots. Those popular Scandinavian Rya rugs are usually woven with the Giordes knot. The same is true of Flossa rugs.

Rugs are woven with rows of knots interspersed with rows of firmly beaten tabby. The number of tabby rows between each pile (or knot) row determines whether the pile will lay flat or stand up. Naturally, the more tabby, the flatter the rug, simply because the pile is less dense and has room to flop over.

Rows of knots are also often used in wall hangings to add a contrast in texture. Depending upon the special look the weaver wants, they can be cut short or left quite long. *(See photographs 155 through 162 on pages 94, 95, and 99 for the rest of the instructions for Strip 3. See photo 148 on page 92 for a completed Strip 3.)*

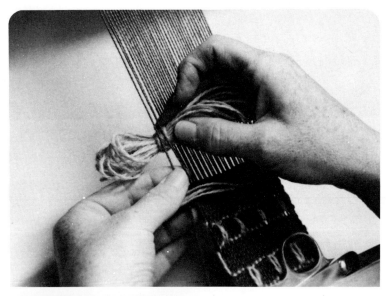

148 Make a butterfly of three strands at once, so that three ends are released at one time. (For Strip 3, green was used for the first row of knots.) Close the shed. On the flat warp, pass the butterfly to the back between the second and third warp end from the left. Hold the ends of the butterfly in front of warp.

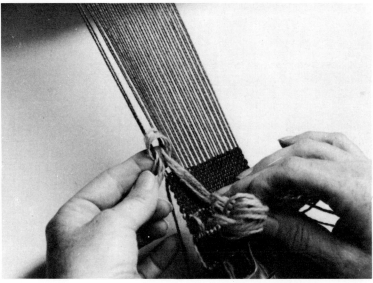

149 Bring the butterfly under two ends (from insertion) to the left, around and over four warp ends to the right. Insert the butterfly again and bring it back under two ends to the left. Bring it back to the surface of the warp in the same space in which it was originally inserted.

150 A **flossa rod** will keep loops an even length. If not available, improvise, as pictured here. Fold a piece of paper between slats (tongue depressors work well).

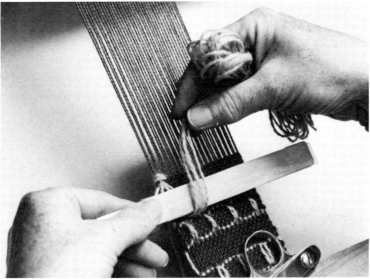

151 Warp the yarn around the rod. Insert the butterfly between the sixth and seventh warp ends. Go back two, and back under two. Repeat across the row.

152 When the row is completed, turn the stick on its side. Use groove to guide scissors and cut loops.

153 Instead of a stick, your thumb can be used for loops. Just be careful to keep the fringe even when cutting.

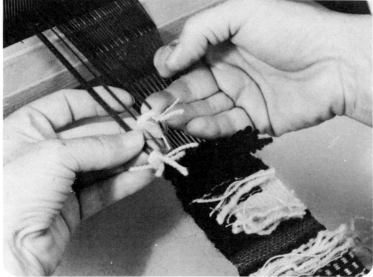

154 After the first row of knots, do a few rows of tabby and do a second row of knots in a contrasting color (yellow). If you don't want to make a butterfly, precut lengths of yarn (see photograph 157) can be placed across four warp ends, turned back under and around, and finished between the second and third warp ends. The same method may be used all across the row.

155 Another form of laid in has the pattern laid in on alternate sheds (followed by background shot as in photograph 137 on page 85). To avoid the "stitch" when alternating row and working on top surface, drop weft butterfly below surface.

156 Bring butterfly up for next row. In this photograph this was not done at the far right and you can see the vertical stitch between laid-in weft rows.

Special Effects

157 To measure precut lengths tor knotting, yarn may be wrapped around any convenient flat surface of desired size. A note pad is used here.

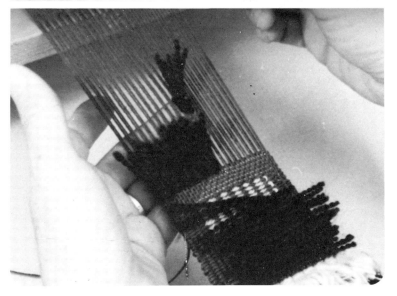

158 For special effects, the knots may be put in "upside down" with the ends coming out above the knot and going up over the warp. Finish Strip 3 with a row of more or these upside down Giordes knots and three inches of plain or tabby weave.

STRIP 4

Tabby ———————

Warp Twill ———————

Tubular Cloth ———————

Double Width ———————

Reverse Layer ———————

Two Layers ———

Tabby with pattern ———————

Reverse Twill ———————

Laid In ———————

Weft Face Twill (orange) ———

Weft Face Twill (yellow) ———

Weft Face Twill (orange) ———

Weft Face Twill (yellow) ———

Weft Face Twill (orange) ———

Right Twill (yellow) ———————

Right Twill (orange) ———————

Left Twill (yellow) ———————

Left Twill (orange) ———————

Soumak ———————

Tabby ———————

STRIP 4

Most of the weaving for the next three steps must be done on a loom with four or more harnesses. There are a few weaves that can be done on two-harness or rigid-heddle looms. If you are working on one of these latter two, the only thing we can suggest is that you read through this section before starting to work and see which instructions can be adapted to you loom.

Warp: 3/2 perle cotton, yellow
Weft: 3/2 perle cotton, yellow and orange
Reed: 12 dent
Sett: 1 per cent (12 epi)
Width: 3 inches (approx.)

ILLUSTRATION 11

STRIP 4

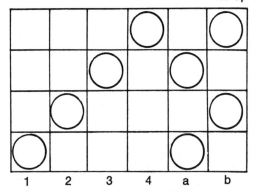

For this strip the threading of the harnesses is exactly as before *(see Illustration 11). Because of the broad range of treadling, it's best to use a "direct tie-up," that is, one treadle to a harness. If the loom has six treadles, the last two are used for tabbys. If it doesn't, you'll have to press down treadles 1 and 3, then 2 and 4, at the same time, to make the tabby sheds.

This is not the most felicitous arrangement for a counter-balanced loom; however, it can be done. Bear in mind that you are weaving upside down. In other words, after you've finished, you'll have to turn the fabric over to get the right side up.

Strip 4 *(see photograph 160 on page 99)* is a joy to work. Not only is it done in those happiest of colors, yellow and orange, but it goes extremely fast. After the slowness of Strip 3, Strip 4 is a breeze.

Twill

(See color photograph 12 facing page 64.)

In plain weave there is an interlacing of each warp and weft thread—over one, under one, and so on. This is not true of **twill.** It's what is called a "float" weave. Weft threads float over two or three warp ends, and they also make progressions like over two, under two, and so forth.

Twills are characterized by a series of diagonal lines, moving either to the right or left, caused by the overlapping of warp ends as the fabric is woven.

Berta Frey, author of *Designing and Drafting for Handweavers* (Macmillan, New York, reissued 1975), once worked out 110 different ways to weave four-harness twill! We're not going to be that generous or laborious, depending on one's point of view. This strip will explore only a few of the basic twills to give you an idea of how it is worked. **Double weave** is included because it is woven on the same threading.

As the weft floats in twill, obviously, so does the warp. Because of this interlacing of more than one warp and weft end at a time, twill is a more compact weave than plain weave. In other words, it takes more weft shots to weave the same amount of fabric than it does in plain weave. This makes it doubly important to do those small samples when using twill in other projects, just to make certain that you have enough weft material.

In this strip we're going to give you an exercise in working from treadling order, tie-up, and draft. The draft and tie-up remain constant for each weave. The treadling order changes. It is ordinarily printed below tie-up. Since Illustration 11 is constant, we've eliminated it below. Just follow the instructions and you should have absolutely no problems. You can reassure yourself by checking on how

your work looks compared to how it looks in the finished strip in photograph 160 on page 99.

ILLUSTRATION 12

TABBY

Illustration 12 is the treadling order for tabby. The 3X alongside the illustration indicates that the complete sequence is to be repeated three times.

After the tabby, make a border by doing two rows of soumak *(see instructions and photographs 97–102 on pages 68 and 69).* Use the orange thread or better still a wool of the same shade.

ILLUSTRATION 13 $2/2 \left(\frac{2}{2}\right)$ LEFT TWILL

Illustration 13 is the treadling order for 2/2 ($\frac{2}{2}$) left twill. The numbers signify that the weft does not intersect with each warp, but passes under two warp ends, then over two. In instructions they may be given either way. One can also do left twill with different proportions ($\frac{1}{3}$, $\frac{3}{1}$).

1. Wind orange thread on a shuttle or make a butterfly of it.
2. Repeat the entire treadling order twice in orange.
3. Repeat the entire treadling pattern twice in yellow. (You have now completed the treadling order four times.)

ILLUSTRATION 16

ILLUSTRATION 14

2/2 $\left(\dfrac{2}{2}\right)$ RIGHT TWILL

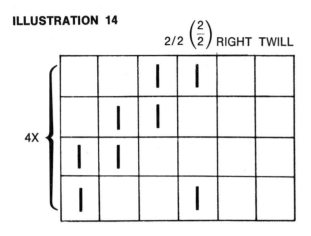

Illustration 14 is for 2/2 right twill. As can be seen, the treadling order is simply reversed, and the resulting diagonals move to the right. Repeat steps 2 and 3 under Illustration 13.

ILLUSTRATION 15

WEFT FACE 1/3 $\left(\dfrac{1}{3}\right)$ TWILL

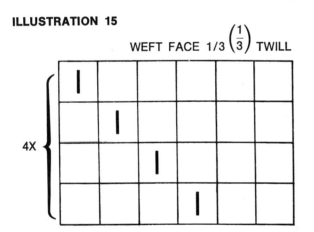

Illustration 15 is for weft face (actually, 1/3 twill) with one weft end going over three warp ends. This means that much more weft than warp will show on the face of the fabric. When the weft does not extend to the last warp thread, catch the end with the shuttle or butterfly to keep the selvedge even. Repeat the treadling order twice in each color.

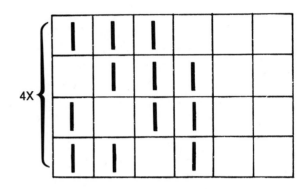

Illustration 16 is for warp face (3/1) twill. It is the reverse of weft face and when weaving one the other appears on the back of the fabric. The instructions are exactly the same as for doing weft face.

Two weft-face shots in orange make a border around a band of tabby (two right after warp face and two just below laid-in).

ILLUSTRATION 17   LAID IN

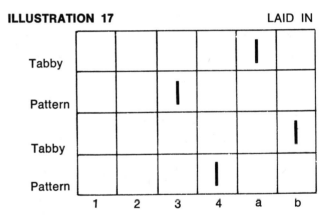

Illustration 17 is the treadling pattern for the four-harness, laid-in pattern. Unlike the *H* in Strip 2 (and the *G* in Strip 3), the pattern shot for the *A* in Strip 4 *follows* the tabby shot instead of preceding it. In addition to that, unlike the others, the same shed is *not* opened for both tabby and pattern shots.

Incidentally, you will notice that the initials "laid in" on these strips are those of the Handweavers Guild of America. In you choose, you can easily substitute your own initials by following any or all of **laid-in** we have given.

With four harnesses, the laid-in pattern takes on a new dimension. It seems to 'float over the tabby when it is woven with treadles 1 or 3 depressed after an *a* tabby shot. The same is true with 2 and 4 after a *b* tabby shot.

159 When weft doesn't extend to the last warp thread, catch the end with the shuttle.

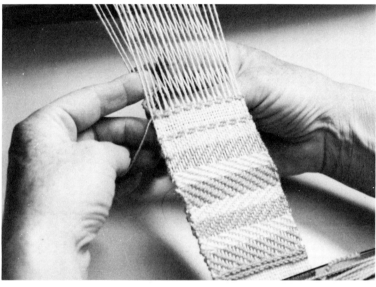

160 When starting a pattern, tuck the end of the pattern yarn in the tabby shed preceding the pattern shot. For the "A" pattern, yarn can be on separate butterflies, netting shuttles, or on one of each.

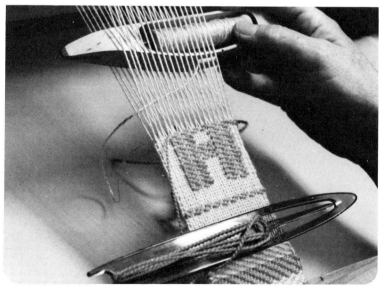

161 The pattern on treadle 3 follows an *a* tabby shot. The pattern on treadle 4 follows a *b* tabby shot.

ILLUSTRATION 18

LAID-IN: Variation

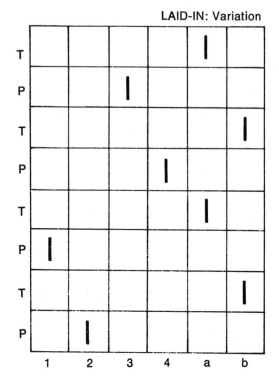

ILLUSTRATION 19

REVERSE TWILL

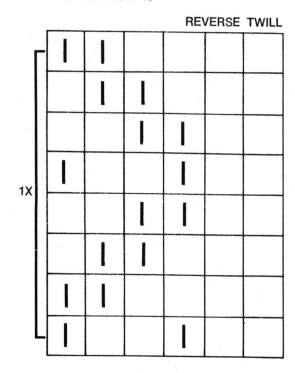

Illustration 18 is the treadling order for an interesting variation on laid-in. In this case, treadles 1 and 3 alternately follow the *a* tabby shots, and 2 and 4 the *b* tabby shots.

Four harness **laid-in** forms the basis for four-harness tapestry techniques. The most famous of these was developed by the English artist and weaver, Theo Moorman. On harnesses 3 and 4, she uses extremely fine warp threads which almost disappear in the heavier weft pattern yarns. For her ground weft (for background and tabby shots) she usually uses a very fine linen.

Weave a few rows of tabby.

Illustration 19 is the treadling order for **reverse twill.** Resembling horizontal chevrons, this band of reverse twill is woven with orange weft thread. It is followed by a few more rows of plain tabby.

ILLUSTRATION 20

COMBINATION TABBY AND PATTERN

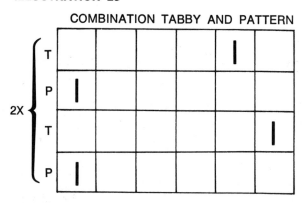

Illustration 20 is the treadling order for a combination of tabby and pattern. The pattern is laid in when harness 1 is lifted. Both tabby and pattern are done with the orange thread. Repeat the treadling order twice.

This combination weave makes a beautiful decorative border for placemats and shawls. As an overall weave it's especially effective when extra warmth is wanted such as in blankets and heavy scarves. As in laid-in, the tabby is beaten back against itself, and the pattern floats over it giving a double thickness.

Weave about ½ inch of tabby in the same thread as the warp.

Double Weave

Double weave is generally woven on a much closer warp than 12 epi. In Strip 4, we employed only the most basic techniques of this fascinating weave. Because it is so interesting and useful, a later section is completely devoted to it. (See Chapter 6, page 148.)

It takes two harnesses to weave plain cloth but on four harnesses it's possible to weave two layers, making double width or tubular cloth, or the many variations on them. It all depends on the interplay of harnesses and shuttles.

The basic thing to remember in all double weave is that when you are weaving the bottom layer the top layer must be lifted out of the way. As each of the layers will have only half the number of warp ends, the fabric will be much more open than it is for the rest of Strip 4. If you wanted exactly the same consistency you would need twice the number of warp ends sleyed 2 per dent or 24 epi on this 12-dent reed.

ILLUSTRATION 22

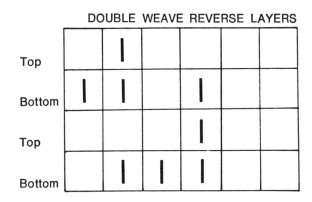

Illustration 22 is the treadling order to **double weave, reverse layers.** As the name implies, it is simply reversing the layers. The top layer is now on harnesses 2 and 4, the bottom layer on 1 and 3. For the top layer treadling use the orange thread and the yellow for the bottom. Continue to do this until the layers appear for about half an inch.

Repeat a few rows of yellow tabby.

ILLUSTRATION 21

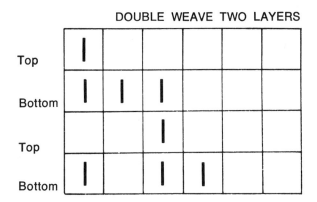

Illustration 21 is the treadling order for **two layers double weave.** The top layer of fabric is woven with yellow on harnesses 1 and 3. The bottom layer is woven with orange on harnesses 2 and 4. *(For instructions, see photographs 162–166 on pages 102 and 103.)*

ILLUSTRATION 23

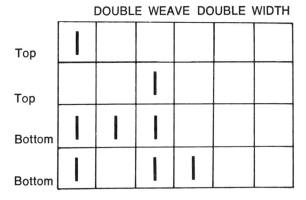

Illustration 23 is the treadling order for **double weave, double width.** This is an extremely useful weave which makes it possible to weave fabric twice the weaving width of your loom. This is why it is particularly useful for making blankets, table cloths, and drapery fabrics. All of the weaving is done with one shuttle (orange thread in Strip 4), so that the front and back will match each other in color when unfolded and the weaving be continuous across the doubled width of the fabric.

The top layer is woven in both directions before repeating on the bottom layer.

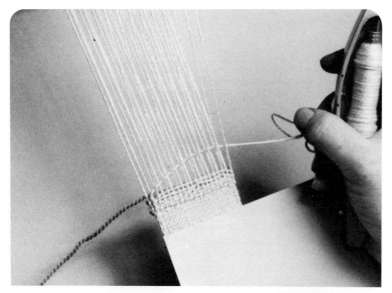

162 Lift harness 1. With yellow thread, weave from left to right.

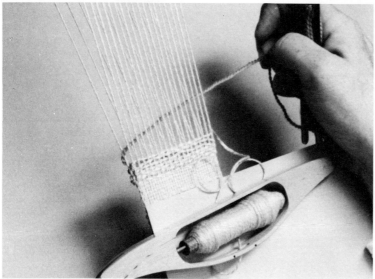

163 Lift harnesses 1 and 3 (tabby *a*, if you have it) which constitute the top layer, *plus harness 2*, the bottom layer. Weave from left to right with the orange thread.

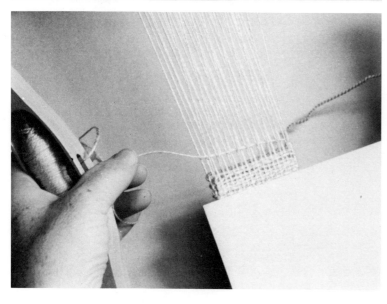

164 Lift harness 3 and weave from right to left with the yellow thread. Notice that this is bringing the yellow thread back to its starting selvedge.

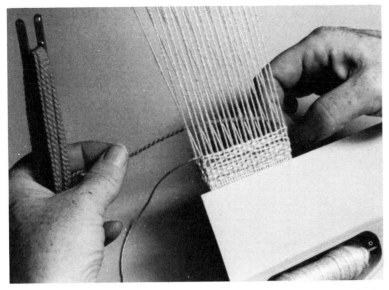

165 Lift harnesses 1 and 3 *plus harness 4* and weave from right to left with the orange thread back to its starting selvedge. Repeat steps 162 through 165 for desired length.

166 After a few repeats of the four steps above, two layers will start to appear. Notice the looseness of the weave compared to the fabric below it. This is because you are only using half the warp ends for each layer.

167 This is double width double weave with the opening on the right side. To have the opening on the right, start weaving at the left selvedge. Weave left to right and back to left on the top layer (treadles 1 and 3). Left to right and back to left on the bottom layer (treadle 2 plus tabby *a*, then 4 plus tabby *a*). If you don't have the tabby, it's treadling 1 and 3, which are the top layer, plus 2 then 4). After a few rows, the opening begins to appear.

Do ½ inch of tabby in the same thread as the warp.

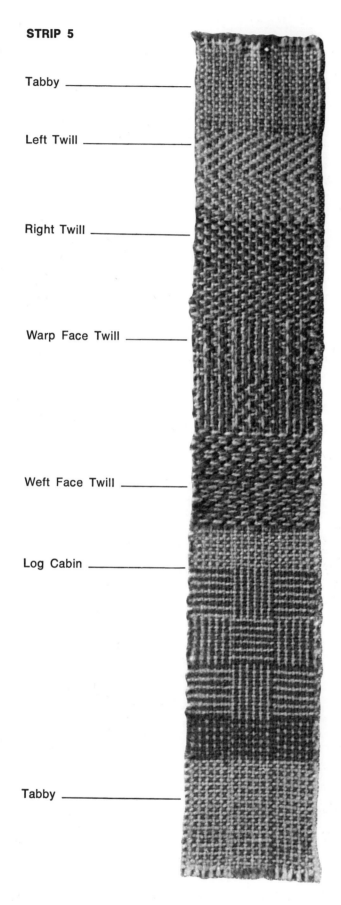

Tabby _____

Left Twill _____

Right Twill _____

Warp Face Twill _____

Weft Face Twill _____

Log Cabin _____

Tabby _____

Tubular Cloth

Tubular cloth is woven with only *one shuttle. (See Illustration 21 on page 101 for the treadling order for tubular cloth.)* Use the orange shuttle. It is essentially two layers closed at the sides and open at the top and bottom. To close the top and bottom of tubular cloth, start with a tabby shot, do the tubular weave, and end with a tabby shot. This weave is particularly suitable for pillow covers, purses, and bags of all kinds.

Finish Strip 4 with tabby and whatever types of twill you find pleasing, until the desired length of eighteen inches is reached.

Before removing Strip 4 from the loom, advance the warp sufficiently to leave enough on the loom to extend through the reed.

The warp for Strip 5 is going to be tied onto the existing warp.

STRIP 5

The warp for this strip is the first one you will do that has more than one color. We're going to use it to take the opportunity to teach you three new warping techniques: (1) winding on a warping board with two colors, (2) tying a new warp to the end of one already on the loom, and (3) lacing to tie-on rod with a string.

Strip 5 is going to use one new weave that can be done on both two- and four-harness looms. Its name is **Log cabin** and it has enjoyed enormous popularity for generations.

Log Cabin

Log cabin is an irresistible combination of a weave: it's easy to do on any loom with a simple shedding device and it also presents utterly fascinating design possibilities. It can be used as an overall pattern or limited to borders. The pattern shifts simply by changing the sequence of colors. Interesting variations can be introduced by using different filling materials. For our purposes we're sticking to our good old 3/2 perle cotton in orange and red for both weft and warp.

Warp: 3/2 perle cotton, orange and red
Weft: 3/2 perle cotton, orange and red
Reed: 12 dent
Sett: 12 epi
Width: 3 inches (approx.)

Winding Two Colors on a Warping Board

Tie red and orange threads to the first peg on the board (upper lefthand corner of the board). Wind warp as shown in photographs 168 and 169. At the end of the twelfth length (or six times around the pegs with both threads at once), change the sequence at the cross, so that *orange goes over then under and red goes under then over.* At the end of the next twelve, change back to the original sequence.

After completely winding the warp on the board, tie off the cross, chain as you remove the warp, and put in lease sticks as usual.

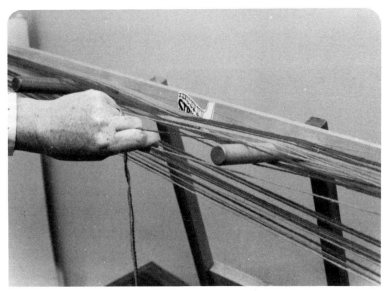

168 Holding both spools at one time in one hand, separated by your fingers, wind the red thread over the second peg and the orange thread under it.

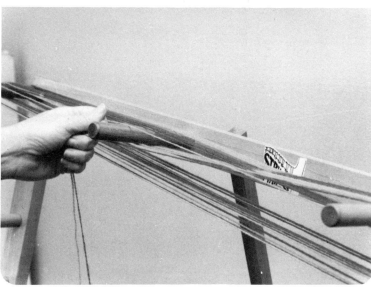

169 Before the next peg, flip the threads so that orange goes over it and red under it. This forms the cross.

Tying a New Warp onto an Old One

One of the most important advantages of tying on a new warp to one already on the loom is that it saves thread. There is obviously far less wastage (fewer *thrums*). Another great advantage is that it saves work, especially if a complicated threading is to be repeated, because it has already been proven correct on the older warp.

As before, tie the lease sticks holding the chain to the breast beam. Cut the warp ends and begin tying one end at a time to the ends Strip 4, which have already been cut on your side of the beam.

The **Weaver's knot** is used to tie the new warp to the old. This versatile knot is also used to repair broken warp ends and to make substitutions of new ends for existing ones when color sequences should change. It may be tied of thick and thin strands and clipped close. As long as it is pulled from both ends, it will hold.

If a mistake is made in the knot, it can easily be untied. All you have to do is pull one end straight and slide the other off. (For the sake of clarity, heavy wool yarn is substituted for the 3/2 perle cotton in the instruction photographs.)

170 Fold back one end of the old warp and hold the loop in your hand.

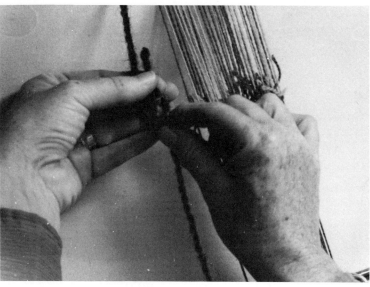

171 Insert the new warp end through the loop made of the old one, coming up from back.

172 Bring the new warp out to a side, make a loop, and bring the end under the loop of the old warp.

173 Bring the new warp end up over the old loop and insert it into its own loop.

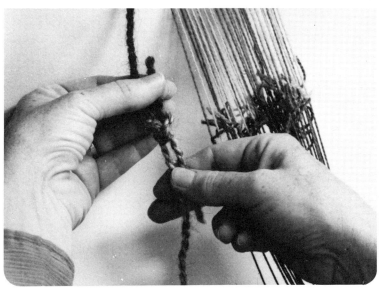

174 Holding *both* ends of the old warp thread and *both* ends of the new warp thread, pull them in opposite directions to tighten the knot.

ILLUSTRATION 24

STRIP 5

Two harness

R		O		R	
	O		R		O

6X   6X   6X

Four harness

R				O				R			
	O					R				O	
		R					O				R
			O					R			O

3X   3X   3X

Illustration 24 shows the drafts for both two- and four-harness looms. They are given in colors rather than numbers because the shifts in color are so important to the Log cabin design. R is for red and O is for orange. Notice the importance of the shifts in color sequence in each bout. For the first, it is red, orange, red, orange for the first twelve threads (6X on the two-harness loom and 3X on the four-harness). We then change to orange, red, orange, red for the next bout, and back to red, orange, red, orange for the last. This means that the twelfth and thirteenth threads are both orange, and the twenty-fourth and twenty-fifth threads are both red.

ILLUSTRATION 25

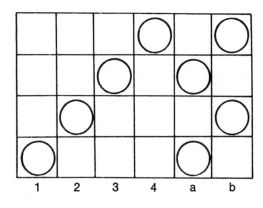

1   2   3   4   a   b

Illustration 25 is the tie-up on a four-harness Jack loom. For a two-harness loom, it's merely 1-2, 1-2 all across the width.

When all the new warp ends have been tied with weaver's knots to the old warp ends, start easing them through the dents in the reed and the heddles as you wind the new warp onto the warp beam.

As the knots approach the back beam, have heavy paper ready to wind onto the warp beam so that the new warp is kept untangled.

Unbraid the chain as you need more warp. As the end of the warp reaches the breast beam, bring up the cloth rod. You could directly tie on as you did with the first warp, but why not learn a new technique? It gives you an alternative that you might actually prefer, and it also wastes less material. Instead of tying directly, lace the warp to the cloth rod. *(See photographs 177–182 on pages 109–111.)*

Begin Strip 5 by doing 3″ of tabby using the orange weft.

Follow with 1″ of tabby using the red weft.
You are now ready to start log cabin.

1. Continue weaving alternating orange and red for the next twelve rows.
2. Alternate red and orange for another twelve rows.
3. Repeat steps 1 and 2 for desired length.

Log cabin can be done on a two-harness loom by doing the whole strip in it. If you have a four-harness loom, finish the strip with twill treadlings.

175 Ease the knots through the dents and heddles as you wind slowly onto the warp beam.

176 Paper being wound onto warp beam as the knots of the new warp approach the back beam. (Notice that there is a sectional warp beam on this loom. *It is not used for this project.*)

177 Tie each ¾-inch section of the warp ends into a knot (if the warp was a wider one, you would tie each bout, or one-inch section, into a knot). Tie the end of a substantial string to the cloth rod. This string should be more than long enough to pass through all the knotted sections of the warp and should be tied off to the rod at the end of them. Pass this string through the center of the first knotted section and loop it around the cloth rod. Repeat until you've laced all the section to the rod.

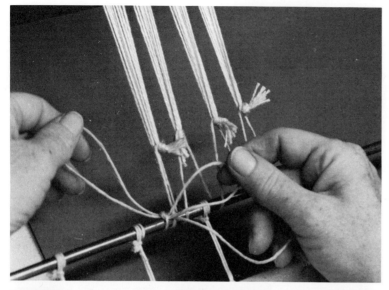

178 With a slip knot, tie the end of the cord to the rod.

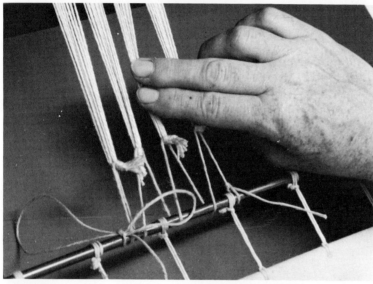

179 With your fingers, gently press down on each section of the warp to test for tension.

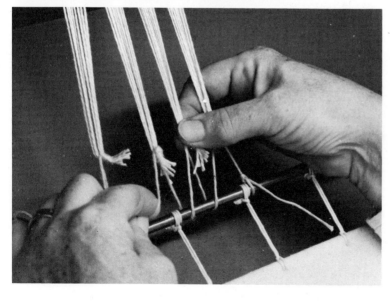

180 To adjust the tension, pull the loose section towards the rod with one hand, while tightening the lacing cord by pulling it firm with the other hand. Continue across the warp.

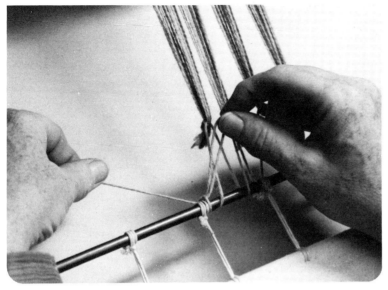

181 When all the sections are evenly taut, pull out the slip knot holding the cord to the cloth rod and retie it securely to the rod, making certain to continue to maintain the section tensions.

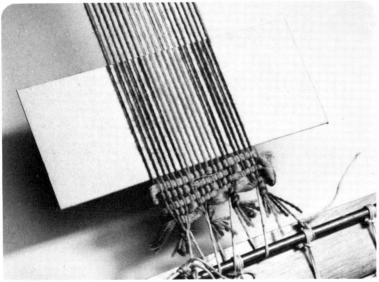

182 Start weaving on the new warp in the usual manner with thrums or rag strips. If a fringe is desired, open a tabby shed and insert into the warp a piece of cardboard the width of the fringe. Push it down toward the strips. Close that shed and begin the actual weaving.

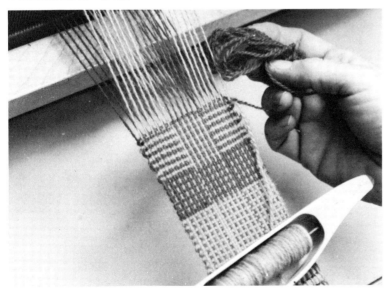

183 Doing Log cabin on Strip 5, alternate orange and red weft shots for 12 rows, *then red and orange for 12 rows.* That's 6 shots of each thread for each sequence of 12.

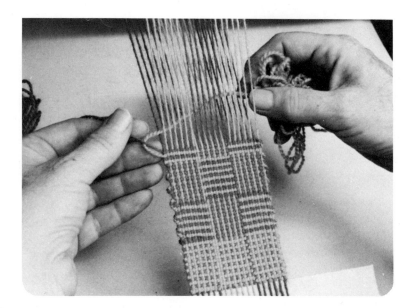

184 Interlocking the two colors at the selvedge to keep edges even.

ILLUSTRATION 26

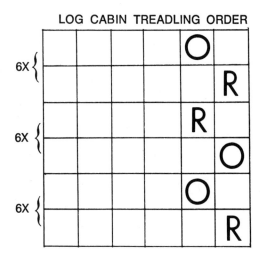

LOG CABIN TREADLING ORDER

Illustration 26 is the treadling pattern for Log cabin on the tabby treadles with two shuttles. If you don't have tabby treadles, make the easy transposition we've already told you about to whatever loom you're working on.

The treadling order immediately indicates that you alternate weft color sequences after every twelfth shot because letters (for the colors) are used as symbols instead of serifs. Notice that the same colors are adjacent after every twelfth shot.

Finish Strip 5 by trying various twill weaves, alternating the color throughout.

If you're working on a two-harness loom, the twills cannot be done. Finish the strip by trying some leno (*see photographs 103–107 on pages 70–71*) and bouquet lace (*see photographs 117–122 on pages 75 and 77*). They're wonderfully effective on a two-color warp.

ILLUSTRATION 26A

TREADLING ORDER WEST FACE
ON LOG CABIN THREADING

Illustration 26A is the treadling order for weft-face twill on log cabin threading.

STRIP 6

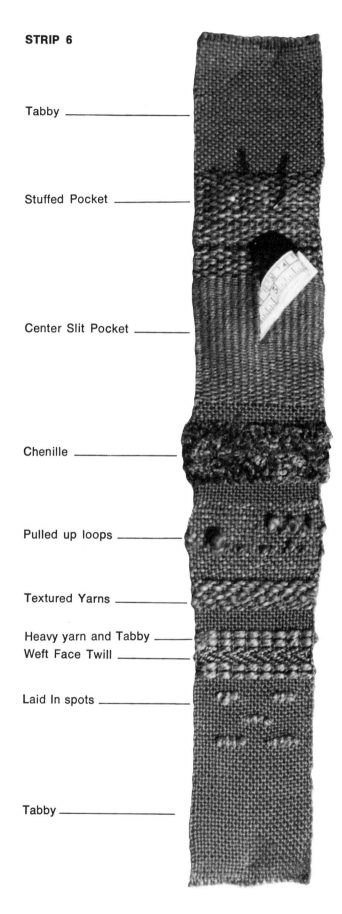

Tabby _____

Stuffed Pocket _____

Center Slit Pocket _____

Chenille _____

Pulled up loops _____

Textured Yarns _____

Heavy yarn and Tabby _____
Weft Face Twill _____

Laid In spots _____

Tabby _____

STRIP 6

Warp: 3/2 perle cotton, red
Weft: 3/2 perle cotton, red; small amounts of
      textured yarns, threads, and fibers
Reed: 12 dent
Sett: 12 epi
Width: 3 inches (approx.)

The warp is threaded on the loom in the same 1-2-3-4 progression as previously used. For this strip, a direct-action tie-up with tabbys was used. *(See Illustration 4 on page 32.)*

Now that you've assimilated all the techniques in the other strips, you can enjoy yourself. This strip is a combination of the techniques learned so far plus a few more such as the **center-slit pocket** *(see pages 116 to 118)*. Follow along with us or do your own thing.

We do think you'll enjoy some of the variations we've laid out, but if you're in a mood for adventure do whatever appeals to you. You'll find that simply using all the threads, yarns, and fibers you have around for the weft, rather than only 3/2 perle cotton, is going to give your weaves a new look that's both refreshing and exciting.

We started with 3″ of tabby, using the same red 3/2 perle cotton for both weft and warp.

Inlaid Spots

Instead of laying in whole areas, laying in spots of color and texture can lend great dash to plain weave fabrics. *(See photographs 185–187 on page 114.)*

Inlaid spots can be done on a two- or four-harness loom. The rest of our suggestions require four harnesses.

185 Textural excitement with inlaid spots in plain weave. 1½-inch lengths of cotton rug yarn in contrasting color folded in three and laid in tabby shed before the shot.

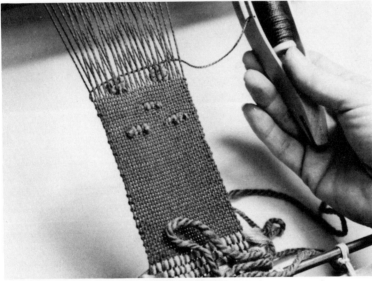

186 After spots are laid, inset tabby shot in the same shed. Close and beat hard.

187 Next two tabby shots are beaten hard to hold spots in place. After that, tabbys are beaten easily to even up the web.

188 Combining a variety of treadling orders with a variety of colors and textured wefts to develop interesting borders and overall patterns. Combinations of dull and shiny or thick and thin add an exciting novelty to the patterns. Here, a wool and rayon blended textured yarn is used. Notice how the weft-face, at top, emphasizes the texture, while the tabby above it, with same filling material, reduces it to a speckled effect.

189 Additional textural embellishments are accomplished by pulling up loops at random while weaving.

ILLUSTRATION 27

STRIP 6

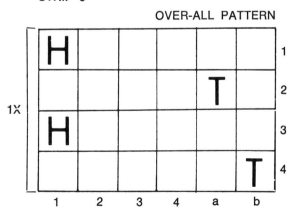

Illustration 27 is the treadling order for an overall pattern combining a heavy yarn (H) and regular tabby (T) with the weft the same as the warp. When finished, the heavy yarn will seem to float above the web. You might do two rows.

Tubular Weave

ILLUSTRATION 28

TWILL
(with contrasting color and texture)

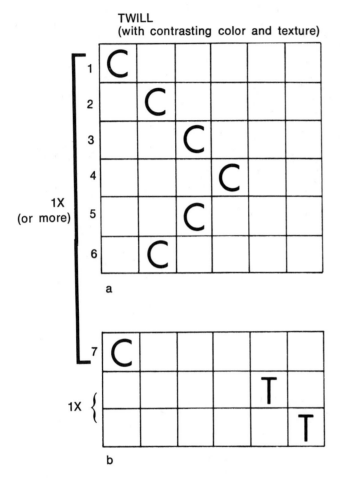

a

ILLUSTRATION 29

TUBULAR WEAVE

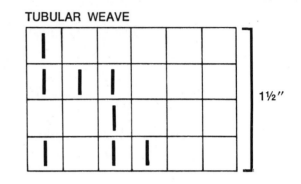

1½″

b

CENTER SLIT POCKET

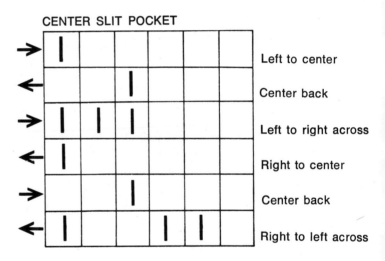

Left to center

Center back

Left to right across

Right to center

Center back

Right to left across

Illustration 28 is the treadling order for a weft-face twill done with a contrasting color and texture (C). We suggest you do treadling 1 to 7 one time, but you can do it more. Remember always to end with the two tabby shots.

Illustration 29 shows the treadling orders for tubular weave and the center-slit pocket. This is a project that all people with four-harness looms (or more) should try. It's fun and it's easy. The pocket is actually a version of the double weaves we did on Strip 4, only this time the opening is in the center instead of on the side.

Start by weaving tubular for 1½″ *(see Strip 4, page 104)*. Beat hard so that this pocket will be solid enough to hold things. The result will be a weft-face fabric on this threading.

190 To start a **center-slit pocket,** lift harness 1 and weave to the center of the warp. Close the shed and beat. Lift harness 3 and weave back to the selvedge. This is done from left to center and back to left. Here, a package of thread serves as a shuttle.

191 Lift harnesses 1 and 3 plus 2 and weave straight across from left to right. Close the shed and beat.

192 Lift harness 1 and weave from right to center. Close the shed and beat. Lift harness 3. Weave back to the right selvedge.

193 Lift harnesses 1 and 3 plus 4. Return to the left selvedge by weaving across the bottom layer. Repeat steps 190 through 193 for the length of the slit.

194 Slit will show after a few complete rows have been woven.

195 For a colorful effect, weave slit pocket with three or four different strands of thread at one time. Not only does this add interest, but it saves time. With this trebled weft, the weaving is speeded up. With small pieces like this, all the threads can be held in your hand and fed through your fingers.

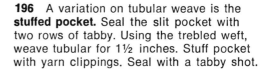

196 A variation on tubular weave is the **stuffed pocket.** Seal the slit pocket with two rows of tabby. Using the trebled weft, weave tubular for 1½ inches. Stuff pocket with yarn clippings. Seal with a tabby shot.

197 Finish Strip 6 with tabby same weft as warp. The stuffed pocket makes a good pin cushion.

SMALL HANGINGS

These narrow warps are just right for making small hangings that are quick to do and great fun. They provide you with an excuse to apply all the techniques we've been doing in the strips and to do exciting things like double weave with one pattern on the bottom layer and things like leno *(see page 70)* and bouquet lace *(see page 75)* on the top layer. (See photographs 208–212 on pages 124 and 125.)

What's even nicer, these little hangings make marvelous gifts and, if you're of a mind, good sale items.

If you want to do a more impressive hanging, simply put on a wider warp. The same instructions apply no matter what width you choose to use. The width of your loom is the only thing limiting the size of your hangings.

Finishing a Hanging

Wrapping is a good way of finishing off a hanging. It adds color and enables the weaver to make a fringe without knots; as you'll see later, it can also be used in the body of a hanging. *(See photographs 198–202 for instructions.)*

Another method of finishing uses bamboo sticks at the top and bottom of hangings to give them support and to provide a convenient rod from which to suspend them. Metal rods and other types of decorative sticks can be inserted in the same way. *(For instructions, see photographs 203–209 on pages 122 and 123.)*

If you're planning to do another hanging on the same warp, you should insert a cardboard the width of the fringe you're planning for it before beginning to weave. *(For instructions on how to insert the cardboard, see photograph 182 on page 111.)*

To do a hanging with dried flowers inserted in it, do a few rows of **two layers,** leaving both sides open. Reverse the layers and weave a few more rows.

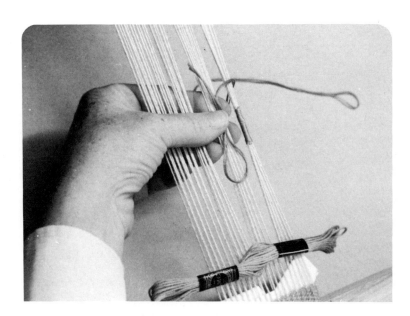

198 Leave an unwoven piece of warp between the last piece woven and the start of new hanging. With the material to be used for wrapping (here, doubled), make a loop slightly longer than the area to be wrapped. Place the loop over the section of the warp to be wrapped. Leave the loop down, cut end up.

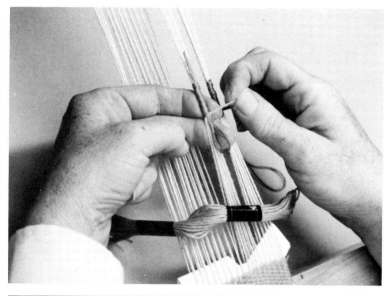

199 Starting at the top, wind the wrapping thread around the warp ends. The wraps should lay smoothly, each turn touching but not overlapping the previous one.

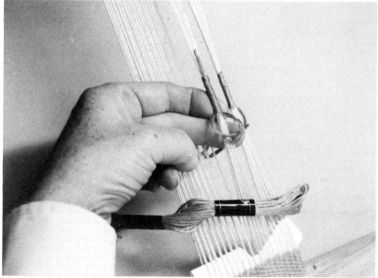

200 When the desired area has been wrapped, cut the wrapping material and place this new end through the loop at the bottom.

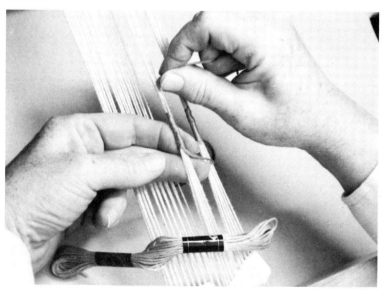

201 Pull up the end at the top until the loop at the bottom with the other end through it is pulled into the wrapped area. Be firm but gentle, taking care not to pull the whole thing apart.

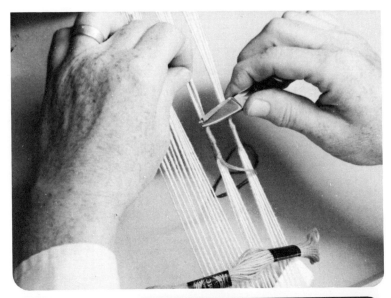

202 Clip off excess wrapping thread above and below the wrapped area. Repeat steps 198 through 202 across the warp. The portion between thrums and wrapping will be your fringe when you remove hanging from the loom.

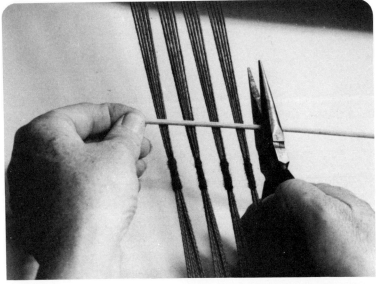

203 Cut off a piece of bamboo skewer slightly wider than the warp so that the ends will protrude at both sides.

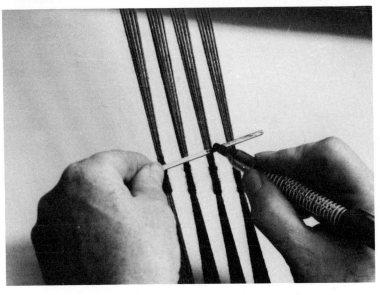

204 Paint cut bamboo stick with a permanent ink marker. (The color is your choice.) Insert stick in the 2–4 tabby shed and start weaving as usual with the 1–3 tabby shed.

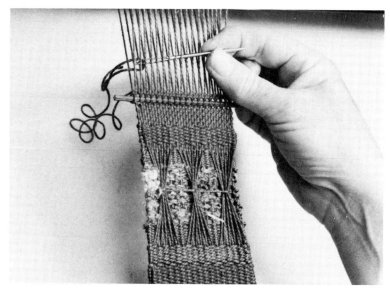

205 When hanging is completed, repeat steps 203 and 204, ending with two rows of tabby. Cut the weft, leaving about twelve inches, and thread this end in a needle. Open the next shed. Place the needle in it, bringing it up and out at the center of the warp.

206 Push the needle through the warp under the stick.

207 Knot the threaded warp end around the stick and cut off the excess. This will provide string to hang the piece.

208 To vary your hangings you might try using clasped weft on the bottom layer of double weave, instead of plain weave. (See photographs 126 and 127 on page 80.) Different textured strands add interest and heighten the effect. Do bouquet lace (see photographs 117 through 120 on pages 75-76) on the top layer, using one of the wefts from the bottom layer to make ties. This anchors the top to the bottom. Continue clasped weft on bottom layer.

209 Weft can be wrapped twice around the bouquet warp ends to hold the bouquet lace securely.

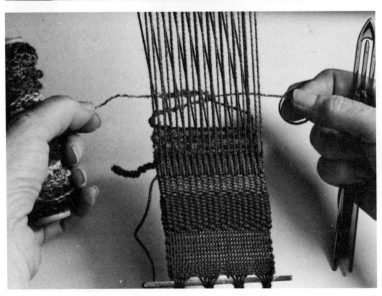

210 Clasped weft being woven on bottom layer of double weave.

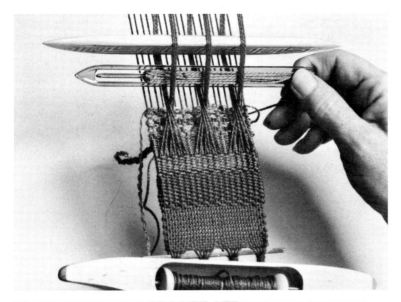

211 With clasped weft on the bottom layer, do leno (see photographs 103 through 105 on pages 70 and 71) on the top layer. Use a pick-up stick to hold the leno twists, and use one of the clasped-weft threads in the shed to hold the leno.

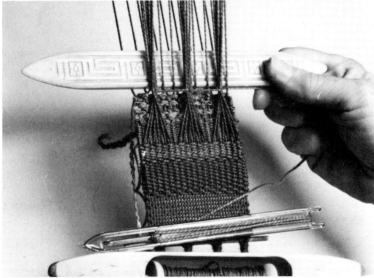

212 Use a pick-up stick to push the clasped weft into place for a few rows after the leno twist.

213 After completing the hanging, apply glue to the edge of the weft to prevent unraveling.

6 OTHER WARPS, OTHER WEFTS, OTHER WEAVES

She had been weaving for thirty years and was a regular at the convergences of the Handweavers Guild of America. Convergence is the name given to a national conference of weavers, complete with seminars and workshops led by some of the world's foremost practitioners.

She told me: "I come to these meetings mostly for the workshops. I've been at my loom for a long time, but there's always something new to learn. That's what's so exciting. It's both the oldest and the newest of the crafts. You can spend your whole life doing nothing but exploring the possibilities of something like the twill progression, or you can go on to something so innovative that it just staggers you. It all depends on the kind of person you are, what you want out of your weaving, what you're in it for. Me—I love mixing up all the olds and the news and seeing what comes out. You'd be surprised. Why, sometimes, I've even surprised myself."

If you've been following along with the strips and hangings, you've already learned enough to branch out and do all kinds of wonderful things on your own. It's only a question of putting a warp on and letting yourself go. Perhaps you'd rather start by using one of the drafts in Chapter Three to do your own drawdown and treadling order. Go ahead. It takes no more than a sheet of graph paper. For those who want to learn a few more weaves, the following are among the most versatile and popular.

ROSEPATH

There's every reason in the world for **rosepath** to enjoy its enormous popular appeal. It's a weave that has instant design possibilities. It can be woven as a twill (it's actually a version of twill), or as colonial overshot, with a separate pattern and tabby wefts (more about this a little later), or as the basis for four-harness tapestry.

The pillows *(see color photographs 13 to 23 facing pages 65 and 128)* were all woven using the same threading and tie-up. For the exact draft for threading and tie-up, see Illustration 5 on page 34.

The warps were made of:

· Brown 3/2 perle cotton sett 12 epi
· Silver 5/2 perle cotton sett 15 epi
· White four-ply orlon knitting yarn sett 12 and 10 epi

Rosepath is a marvelous weave with which to experiment. Because the possibilities in design are so vast, it's best to do a drawdown before actually beginning. Illustrations 5, 6, and 7 on pages 34, 35, and 36 give you some idea of how patterns shift simply by changing the treadling order without any new tie-ups or threading.

For a start, why not put on a nice wide warp and do a pillow following the treadling in Illustration 5. You could use the same yarn for both the warp and weft and still enjoy the textural subtleties. It might be fun to add a border in another color. For this pattern effect, use a pattern weft slightly heavier than the warp and again the same thread as the warp for the tabby weft. Work with a butterfly and shuttle or two shuttles. In putting in the pattern, a tabby shot follows each pattern shot. You can see this clearly in Illustration 7 on page 36. As a matter of fact, this treadling order will produce a lovely border for your pillow.

The pattern is also easy to do with a direct tie-up by lifting one harness at a time for the pattern shot and following with a tabby shot. The same pattern harnesses can be lifted any number of times (or two at a time if you are following Illustration 7 on direct tie-up) so long as a tabby always follows the pattern pick (or shot).

The banners (see color photograph 27 facing page 33) are not only a vivid study in color, but they also serve as a weaving exercise. In addition to being handsome, they are good points of reference to hang in your workshop, for they illustrate many variations that can be done in rosepath.

Warp: cottolin used double, violet, blue, green,
      yellow, orange, red;
      8/4 cotton, black, gray, white
Weft: same as the warp plus wool Rya yarn
Reed: 12 dent
Sett: 12 epi

Depending on the length and width of the fabric you wish to weave, calculate the amount of thread necessary for the hangings (plus waste allowances) and have it on hand.

The warp is the same for the three banners and the framed piece (color photograph 24 facing page 128). Each of the colors is approximately 2" or 24 warp ends. There are six colors and seven stripes (three black, one at each end; one in the center,

and two each of gray and white). Each of the stripes is ¾" or 9 warp ends wide, except the black selvedge stripes, which are 12 ends each including a waste allowance. It needn't be the usual 10% if you use a **Temple** to maintain the width. There is a great tendency to "draw in" ((narrow) in Rosepath.

Illustration 30 (see next page) is the draft for the three banners. In each case, thread stripes and bands as separate units, finishing required repeats of one sequence before starting the next.

In winding the warp, be sure to keep an accurate count. It's essential to the pattern that there be no variation in the width of stripes.

The threading and tie-ups are those shown in Illustration 5 on page 34.

Begin weaving the long banner with tabby to "square the design." This means you use the same threads and order of colors for the weft as you used in the warp. The weft exactly duplicates the warp. You begin with ¾" of black, then 2" of violet and so on, ending with 2" of red and ¾" of black.

Next, follow the treadling order in Illustration 5 on page 34 and again square the design but start with the red. Do not repeat the black stripe that separates it from the tabby square.

End the banner by squaring with twill (treadle 1, 2, 3, 4, 1, 2, 3, 4).

The entire banner is woven with the same threads for the warp and weft. There are no tabby shots between the pattern shots.

The hanging with the long tails of solid color is woven with the Illustration 5 treadling and no tabby. Rya yarn was used for the weft seen in the color photograph, but you can use the yarn or the same weft as warp.

The tails are woven with six different butterflies each of the same color as the warp. Violet on violet, orange on orange, yellow on yellow, etc. There is no weaving on the black, gray, and white warp stripes. This is what allows the tails to float independently. At two points the weaving includes the separating stripes (with adjoining color used for the weft) to hold the piece together. The treadling for the tails is the same as for the rest of the piece.

The hanging with the long fringe is one developed on the loom. The treadling is ad lib, that is, no order was designed before the weaving. It's a great

ILLUSTRATION 30

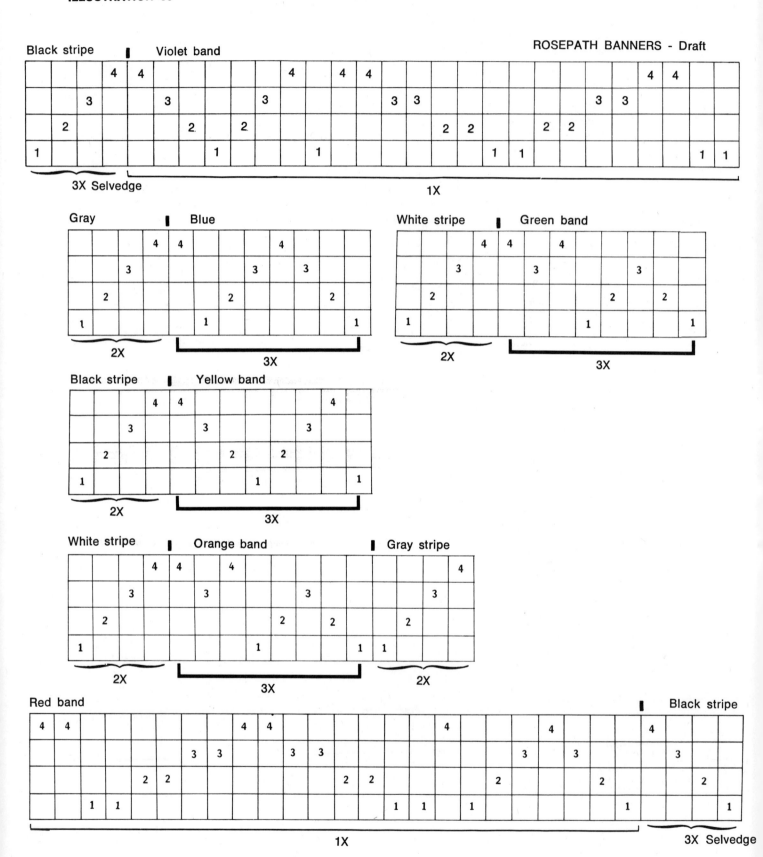

ROSEPATH BANNERS - Draft

128 | OTHER WARPS, OTHER WEFTS, OTHER WEAVES

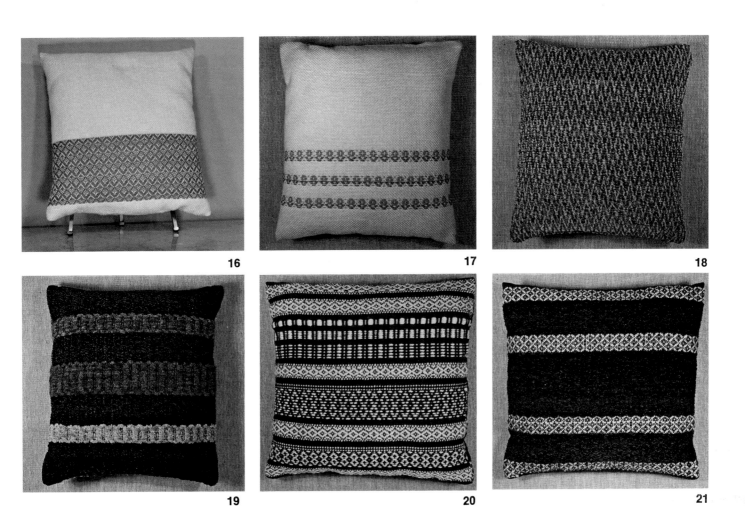

16

17

18

19

20

21

22

23

16–23 All rosepath pillows.

24 Rosepath sampler with clasped weft background.

25 Peter Collingwood's double corduroy woven into a pillow in a blend of natural wools and in bands of color.

26 Rear of one pillow woven in same handspun natural yarns in plain weave. Rear view of other pillow with tabby background. Shot of color laid in on one-harness sheds.

27 Christmas hangings done in double weave.

28 Double weave weed holders.

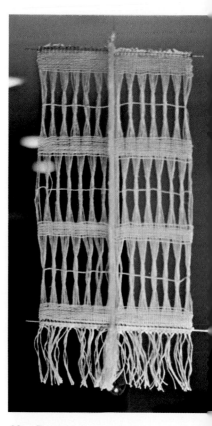

29 Double weave leno hanging.

214 A temple used to maintain width of one of the rosepath banners.

215 Six butterflies of colors matching the colors in the warp stripes used to weave tails.

way to increase your command of pattern on this extremely versatile threading.

The framed piece uses clasped-weft tabby joining at the center of the central black stripe of the warp. Red is under the warm colors (red, orange, yellow) and violet under the others. This is bordered with violet weft straight across for 2″ of tabby at the top and red weft straight across for 2″ of tabby at the bottom.

The blocks of pattern are laid in with butterflies of the same color Rya as that portion of the warp. Each color follows the threading of that stripe. Sometimes this gets rather complicated, necessitating

six shed changes within a single row, but it's such a challenging test of your powers of concentration that we think it will prove very exciting for you.

This is a good time to look at the color photographs of the pillows. Now that you've mastered rosepath, you can appreciate the subtle and bold changes that are wrought by treadling and by the weft materials selected.

DOUBLE CORDUROY

(See photographs 241–261 on pages 141–147.)

Hobbies do become professions and, as we've said, weavers come from every conceivable background. Very few professional weavers start out in their childhoods saying: "When I grow up, I want to be a weaver."

Peter Collingwood studied medicine and was a successful physician before becoming a professional weaver. Whether or not he would have become one of England's most distinguished doctors is impossible to determine; that he did become one of his country's most distinguished weavers is impossible to deny. The Queen recently awarded him the Order of the British Empire in recognition of his contributions to his second profession.

Mr. Collingwood brings his scientific training to weaving. When a technique interests him, he probes, experiments, and researches it, until he has explored all of the possible variations.

He developed **double corduroy** primarily as a method of weaving pile rugs in a short enough time to bring the price down to the point where most of those who wanted to purchase handwoven rugs could afford them. It is one of over 150 techniques that Collingwood explains in his book, *The Techniques of Rug Weaving* (Faber & Faber, Ltd., London), and he has kindly given us permission to describe it in this book.

Many of the techniques that Peter Collingwood uses for his rugs are not specifically rug techniques. The double corduroy can be equally effective for a pillow or bench mat. The latter is a most apt suggestion for weavers. Those loom benches do get hard! A pile weave mat will have a comfortable cushioning feeling—and allow the air to circulate.

Illustration 31 is the draft for double corduroy. As it indicates, each pattern repeat has 20 ends.

This project will be woven with a six-dent reed (6 epi). If we want to do a piece about 16″ wide, that means we need 96 warp ends (16 × 6). However, to do the pattern, repeats of 20 are necessary. The nearest is 100 ends, and we must add 4 ends to reach it.

ILLUSTRATION 31

Collingwood: DOUBLE CORDUROY

4		4		4		4		4											
					3		3		3		3		3						
										2		2		2		2		2	
	1		1												1		1		1

Paddle Warping

In the new warping technique that we are going to illustrate, we'll be winding with a **paddle,** doing 6 ends at a time. The nearest multiple of 6 to 100 is 102. We should add two more ends and thread two ends each into the first and last heddles and dents.

To learn how to warp with a paddle, see photographs 217 to 227 on pages 132 to 135. A three-to-five-yard warp is a good one to use. That means that you'll need 306 to 510 yards of thread to make the warp. Each spool will carry 51 to 85 yards of thread.

To make the warp, use a 8/5 linen thread. The warp will not show, so use two colors, dark and light. As you'll see, this will be very helpful in paddle warping. The only time you cannot do this is if you want to have a solid colored fringe on your double corduroy. Actually, using two contrasting colors can make a very attractive fringe, so consider that alternative.

216 At left, *spool rack* with six spools on it. The threads must feed from the bottom. This is for *paddle warping* with six threads at a time. Next to it, a *warping reel.* Guide string on it has a knot at every yard to measure where the warp is to be wound to give the desired yardage, and also to reach the cross pegs at both the top and bottom of the reel.

Leaning against it, a *paddle* used for paddle warping. Paddles come with from twelve to thirty-two holes for multiple-end warping.

Mounted on top of the reel is a small counter to keep track of the number of turns of the reel.

217 Place spools on spool rack with spools of thread to be threaded through left holes of the paddle on the left (dark thread) and those to go through right holes on the right (light thread).

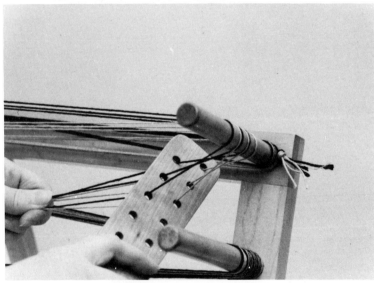

218 Decide on length of warp (three to five yards is good) and wind your guide string on the warping board or reel. Tie six ends coming through the paddle in a knot on the first peg. Start winding. Notice how the colors of warp ends alternate.

219 The left ends (dark thread) go over the second peg, the right ends under it. The separation is natural with the paddle when you hold it with the left threads up.

220 To make the cross, bring the paddle under the third peg. Lift up the alternate (right or light) ends and place them over the peg. The different colors make them easy to pick out.

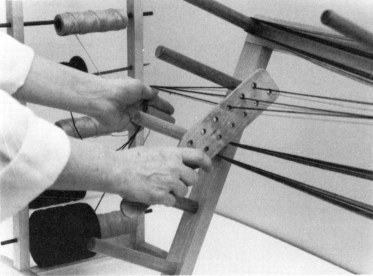

221 Wind the warp on the board or reel. Bring the paddle around the pegs. Hold the warp extended to prevent tangling.

222 If the thread should begin to tangle, hold the paddle in a horizontal position and straighten the ends.

OTHER WARPS, OTHER WEFTS, OTHER WEAVES | 133

223 The entire bout goes around the last peg. Keep count by looping a cord in and out around each individual bout. This is one cord criss-crossing through all the bouts, not a separate one for each. This cord will be useful when it comes to spreading the warp on a raddle later in this exercise.

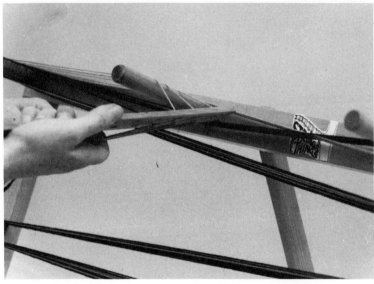

224 On return, remember to maintain cross with light threads going over and under and dark threads going under and over.

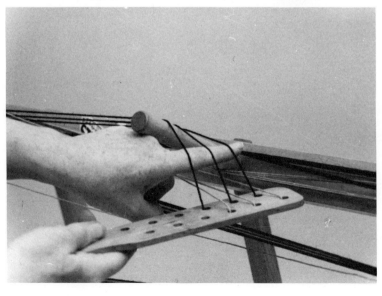

225 On the return, the process is reversed and dark threads are lifted over the appropriate peg. The entire bout goes around the first peg. Repeat the process until the desired number of ends have been wound. For 102 ends, that's eight complete revolutions of the board and one half ending at the last peg on bottom.

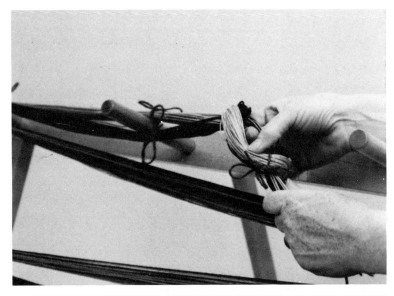

226 Tie four sections of the cross at the top and then make a safety tie (to keep it from unraveling) at the bottom of the warp. Remove the warp from the board by starting to chain at the threading cross at the top.

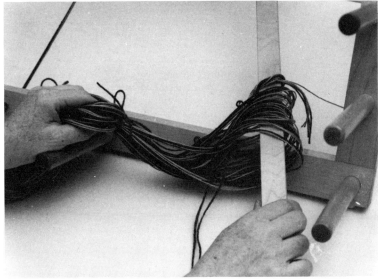

227 When chain reaches last peg on bottom, remove warp from it and place a stick through the loops to help transfer the warp to the loom.

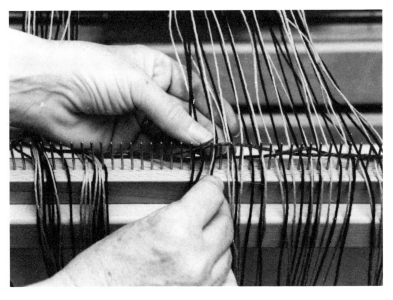

228 Clamp the *raddle* to the *back beam*. Lay warp over the *front beam*. Push the heddles aside, remove reed from the beater. Unchain enough warp for it to reach the back beam. With the warp centered, spread it evenly on the raddle. The looped bouts will help.

OTHER WARPS, OTHER WEFTS, OTHER WEAVES | 135

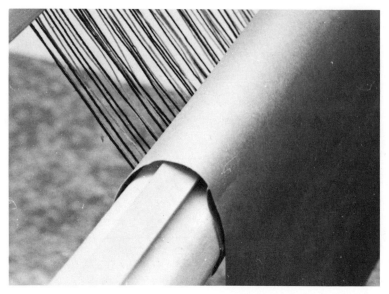

229 Tie a stick (through the bottom loops of the warp) to the warp beam. Start winding on the warp with heavy paper. Exert an even tension by pulling on the warp at the front of loom after each turn of the warp beam.

230 To help maintain this tension, weight the warp in front of the loom with a brick or book.

231 Continue winding on the warp, maintaining as even and tight a tension as is possible. When the threading cross reaches the back of the loom, place the lease sticks through it, tie the sticks, and untie the cross cords.

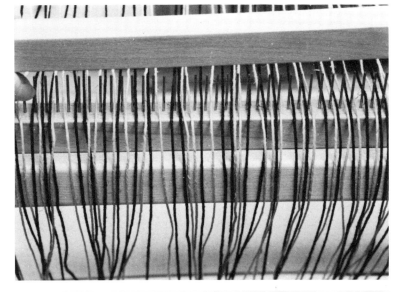

232 After spreading the warp, cap the raddle if it has a cap, or seal it with masking tape.

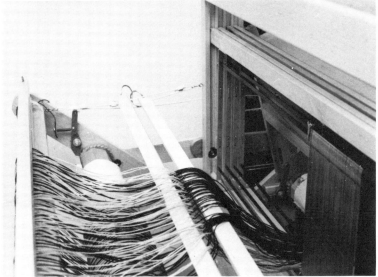

233 Place the lease sticks through the cords tied to the back of the loom or rest them on the wooden supports that stretch from the front to back of the loom. If the lease sticks are not long enough, curtain rods are handy supports.

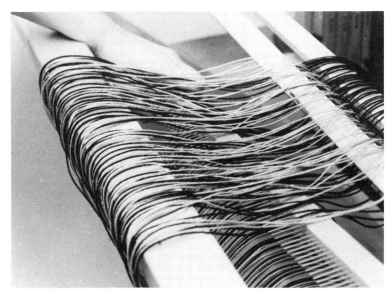

234 Uncap the raddle and remove from the loom by dropping it under the warp.

235 If the front of your loom folds down, do it so that you may sit closer to the heddles while threading them. If the front does not fold down, angle yourself as close to the castle as possible. Bring the warp forward in front of the harnesses.

236 Following the draft (see illustration 30 on page 128), use a threading hook or your fingers to bring the warp through the heddles. Remember to double-thread the first and last heddle. Check each unit of threading for accuracy and tie it into a simple knot.

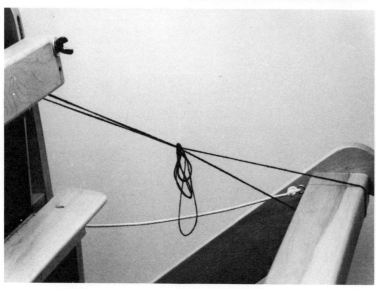

237 If necessary, replace the front of the loom. Tie the beater in an upright position.

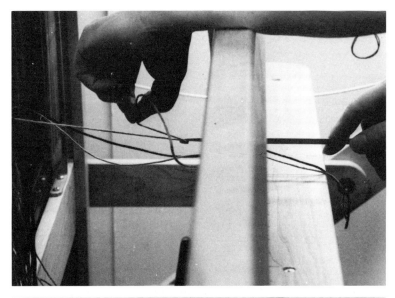

238 One by one, untie the knots in the warp and sley the threads through the reed. Again, remember, two threads in the first and last dents used.

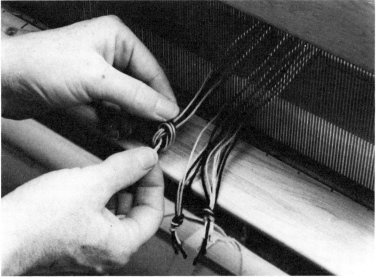

239 Tie a knot at the end of each inch of warp after it has been sleyed through the reed.

240 Lace the warp to the rod of the cloth beam.

ILLUSTRATION 32

ILLUSTRATION 33

TIE UP FOR DOUBLE CORDUROY

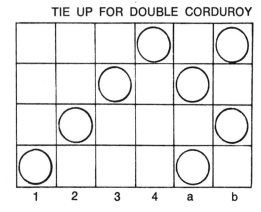

1   2   3   4   a   b

TREADLING ORDER AND SHOT DIRECTION FOR DOUBLE CORDUROY

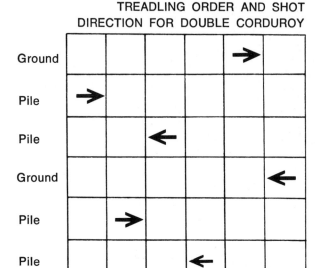

For whole repeat of threading only

Illustration 32 shows the tie-up for double corduroy.

Do the back of the pillow first. *(See color photograph 26 facing page 129.)* Try a heavy homespun rug wool. The blend of natural colors will develop interesting shading when woven. *(See photographs 241 to 244 on pages 141–142.)*

Peter Collingwood's double corduroy is a two-shuttle weave. One is used for the tabby or ground weave, and the other for the pile. There is a special sequence to the weft shots. The one shown here can only be used when full repeats of the 20-end threading draft are used.

Illustration 33 shows the treadling order and the direction of the shots for double corduroy.

You can see from the treadling order that there are long floats in the pile weft of double corduroy. All floats will eventually be cut, but there is a special sequence for cutting some of them during the weaving for the most efficient use of both the technique and the yarns.

Many designs can be worked out in double corduroy by using alternates of different colors in the pile-weft shots. For the pillow in color photograph 25 facing page 129 variety is introduced via the blends of strands wound together, and it is the same blend and color for all of the pile-weft shots.

The blend is composed of:

· 2 strands of 3-ply rug wool, brown
· 1 strand of 3-ply rug wool, gray
· 1 strand of single-ply wool, natural
· 1 Tussah silk thread, natural (to add highlights)

They are all natural (undyed) yarns, and they were wound together on ski shuttles, which are very good choices for this type of weave because they hold a great deal of filling material and they pass through the sheds easily. We would also suggest that you use a rug beater to get extra firmness in the beat. *(See photographs 245–261 on pages 142–147.)*

The other pillow in color photograph 25 is made of two-inch bands of our good old violet, blue, green, yellow, orange, and red. Silks and linens were added to the colored wools. Solid colors are always much more interesting when they are made of blends rather than only one yarn. Six shuttles, one for each shade, were prepared in advance so that work did not have to stop for winding with each change in hue. (For rear of pillow, see color photograph 26.)

241 To work the back of the double-corduroy pillow, start weaving with several rows of heavy yarn. If you wish to have a fringe, insert a piece of cardboard into the tabby shed to maintain space.

242 *Twining* gives a firm edge. Fold a piece of yarn at least four times the width of the warp in half over the left warp end. Cross the two ends of the twining yarn in the space between every other warp end and bring the bottom twining end to the top and the top to the bottom. Keep criss-crossing in this fashion all the way across the warp. Be careful to maintain the warp spacing as it comes from the reed. Groups of four warp ends can also be twined. The twining cross comes between the second and third ends in each group. Twining is a technique used to "spacewarp" ends on looms with no reeds. It is also used by itself as a rug weaving technique.

243 Weave tabby for the entire back of the pillow. To cover the warp and to weave a firm fabric, "bubble" the weft before beating it. This is done by using your finger to make arcs in the weft shot before beating it.

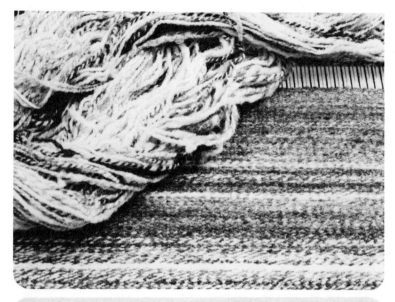

244 The yarn being used is a homespun type that develops interesting shading when woven because of the blends of natural colors in the wool.

245 To work the front of the pillow, a blend of strands of rug wool yarns and Tussah silk threads are all wound together on a ski shuttle. Ski shuttles hold a great deal of yarn and are good choices for this type of weaving.

246 Stick shuttles are also good for this type of weaving. Fully wound, it is easier to pass them through the shed on their sides.

247 Open tabby shed *a* (harnesses 1 and 3) and pass the "ground" shuttle from left to right.

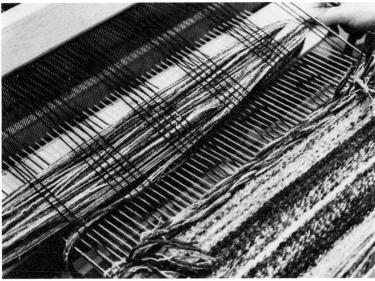

248 Lift harness 1 and pass the "pile" shuttle from left to right.

249 Cut this pile weft about four inches from the right selvedge. The left end can be tucked into the same shed or can be left to be folded in when the pillow is made.

250 Lift harness 3 and pass the pile weft from the right to the left. This shed reaches neither selvedge. Leave a tail at the right side reaching to the selvedge and cut the weft at the left selvedge.

251 Lift tabby *b* (2 and 4). Weave from right to left with the "ground" shuttle. Bubble all tabby shots.

252 When weaving the tabby picks, have the shuttle go under the pile wefts at the selvedges.

253 Lift harness 2 and tuck the tail left on the first weft pick under the raised warp on the right.

254 Pass the pile weft from the left to the right, leaving a small tail at the left. Cut the weft in the space left between the two last warp groups at the right.

255 Lift harness 4 and pass the pile weft right to left. Cut, leaving a small tail at the right, but do *not* cut at the left. Repeat steps 247 through 255 for the entire length of the pillow.

256 For a deeper pile, pull up the loops between the raised warp ends in the pile wefts.

257 After each sequence of pile wefts (complete cycle before repeating), cut the floats.

258 A special tool, available at many weaving supply houses, can lift the floats, facilitating the cutting.

259 Use a rug beater to add extra firmness to the weave.

260 After removing the fabric from the loom, trim the ragged ends to the pile thickness that you desire.

261 When winding a shuttle with a solid color for rug weaving, wind it with groups of various multitextured strands of that color to add depth, interest, sheen, and texture to that color.

DOUBLE WEAVE

Basic double weave has already been covered in the instructions for the strips. There are other, more complicated techniques that are worth trying. They are both challenging and satisfying.

One of the most intriguing develops hangings that have two layers of fabric that intersect at right angles. The results can best be described as three-dimensional crosses.

Using a four-inch warp, in appropriate colors, you can make unusual Christmas tree ornaments. *(See color photograph 27 facing page 129.)*

Weaving a longer strip on the same four-inch warp, "weed holders" prove attractive gifts and, for those with an eye to the economy, successful sale items. *(See color photograph 27 facing page 161.)*

Woven on a wider warp, the "crossed layer" hanging, done with leno, will cast fascinating shadows if placed where the light passes through it. On all counts, it's a wonderfully handsome mobile that will enliven any area. *(See color photograph 29 facing page 129.)*

For this double weave section, we're going to try another way of warping. **Sectional warping** is the best way to put on a long warp by yourself. This is a simple technique and the finished warp will also be easy to work with and have a very good tension.

Sectional-Beam Warping

The method we use here was worked out by Edith Karlin. She finds it so easy to do that she even uses it for short samples. For the short samples, she winds bobbins for each warp end and feeds them through the tensioner *(see photograph)*. Any leftover yarn is then ready to be used as weft in weaving with the bobbin used in a shuttle (or as a butterfly).

Sectional beams *(see photograph 262 on page 148)* are pieces of special equipment which can be fitted on your looms. Other equipment also is necessary: spool rack, tensioner, spools *(see photograph 262),* and a spool winder *(see photograph 26 on page 37)* to wind the yarn on the spools. You should also have two narrow slats that are the same width as the sectional beam.

Sectional beams come with divisions either every one or every two inches. A separate spool of warp yarn is needed for each end per inch that is wound. For example, suppose you're going to do a warp that is 16 epi. For a one-inch sectional beam, 16 spools will be needed. If a two-inch beam is used, you'll have to use 32 spools. This will all become clear in the instructions on sectional warping on pages 148 to 151.

If you have a wide loom (over 32 inches), the two-inch sectional beam is a great time saver. For narrower looms, the one-inch beam might be preferable.

262 To sectional warp, you need a spool rack (left) holding (in this case) 16 spools of thread and feeding the strands from the bottom into a *tensioner* which prepares the warp for the sectional beam. Bring warp ends (threads) through the tensioner in the width to be placed on the beam (one inch in the instruction). It will actually measure less because you must allow for dividers on the sectional beam. Measure the sections to find out the exact width between dividers.

263 Tie the ends of the warp bout into a knot.

264 Tie the warp to the loom cord with a snitch knot. This knot is made by folding back the loop at the end of the cord, creating a second loop on it, and catching the warp bout knot in it.

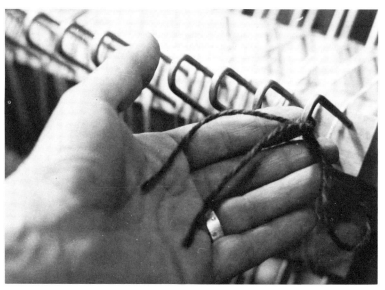

265 Tie a bright-colored string to one of the dividers. As the beam turns, the appearance of the string marks a complete revolution.

266 Keep count of the number of turns by putting a marker (poker chip, match stick, etc.) into a basket. The desired length of the warp determines the number of turns. To find it, divide the circumference of the beam into the length of the warp. Sectional beams come in circumferences from ¼ to 2 yards. As you can see, sectional-beam warping means exactly that. It is put on the beam section by section. After completing the first section (one inch or two inches), start the second section in exactly the same way. For each revolution, remove a marker from the basket. For the third, start replacing them in the basket.

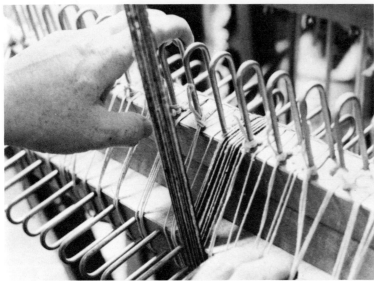

267 To wind the warp ends on, release the brake, sit in front of the beam, and turn it by hand. Make sure the warp section stays within the dividers.

268 When the desired length has been wound, place a piece of masking tape across the front of the bout. Fold the ends under the bout at an angle so that they adhere to the yarn and not to the tape. It makes it easier to remove later.

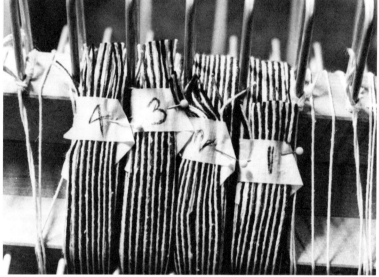

269 Cut the bout above the tape and pin it to the beam. Knot the end of the warp coming through the tensioner and repeat steps 264 through 269.

270 To keep track, number each bout.

271 When desired number has been attained, carefully unpin one section at a time and place it over a flat stick.

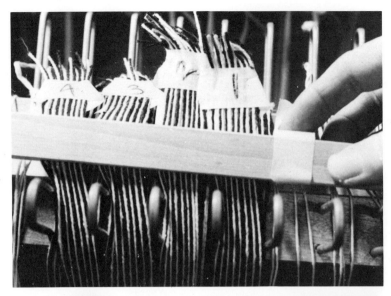

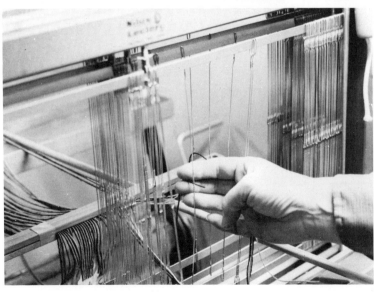

272 Place a second stick over the warp and the first stick, sandwiching the warp between them. Tape the ends of the sticks together.

273 Fold the sticks under the warp and gently bring the whole thing up over the back beam. Place two dowels from the front to the back of the loom and rest the sticks on them.

274 Threading will depend on the draft. We are using the one in Illustration 34 on page 154, with the order of colors reversed at the center. Move to the side enough heddles to complete one section of warp.

275 Bring one section forward, open the tape ends, and, if possible, attach the section with the tape in front of the harnesses. The tape will hold the warp ends in proper sequence for threading. Thread the heddles.

276 Check the threading after each section and knot the bout loosely.

277 Remove the reed from the beater and rest it on the dowels. Sley two ends per dent. After sleying the whole warp, replace the reed in the beater. Tie or lace the warp to the cloth beam.

Double-Weave Hanging

For clarity, we're going to make the warp with two threads: a light and a dark color. (An 8/4 cotton was used for the sample.)

ILLUSTRATION 34

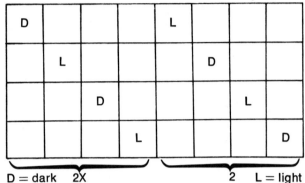

ORNAMENTAL HANGING DOUBLE WEAVE

D = dark 2X   2 L = light

Illustration 34 is the draft for the double weave ornamental hanging. It is warped on a sectional warping beam, but it can be warped in the regular way. "L" represents the light-colored warp ends and "D," the dark. As you can see, each threading sequence is repeated twice and then changed.

Photographs 262–277 on pages 148 to 153 show how to warp with a sectional warping beam.

The first double weave instructions in this section are given with the warp threaded in the two-color sequence on both halves of the width. The result is a crossed hanging which makes a delightful addition to your Christmas tree ornaments.

The tie-up is direct action—harness 1 to treadle 1, 2 to 2, etc. Tabby *a* is 1 and 3. Tabby *b* is 2 and 4.

Warp: 8/4 cotton, two colors
Weft: same plus novelty threads
Reed: 8 dent
Sett: 16 epi (2 ends per dent)
Width: 4 inches (approx.)

OR
Warp: 3/2 perle cotton, two colors
Weft: same
Reed: 12 dent
Sett: 24 epi (2 per dent)
Width: 4 inches (approx.)

Other suitable warp materials are 10/2 linen, 7/2 wool, or rya wool. As two layers will be woven, it's necessary to double the warp ends per inch. For example, 10/2 linen should be used at 12 or 15 epi in regular weaving. The double weave warp should then be 24 or 30 epi sleyed through a 12- or 15-dent reed.

Before beginning, have two stick shuttles wound with the two colors that you are using in the hanging.

The two shuttles are referred to as "L" and "D." Because there are four wings to the hanging, there are eight basic steps to weave completely back and forth on all of them.

1. Lift harness 1. With shuttle L, weave from left selvedge to the center. Bring the shuttle up through the warp. Close the shed by dropping harness 1.
2. Lift 1-3-2, reinsert the shuttle into the shed, and continue to the right selvedge.
3. Lift 1-3-2 and weave from left to center with shuttle D. Bring it up through the warp.
4. Lift 1 and weave to the right selvedge with D.
5. Lift 1-3-4, weave with L to the center, and bring it up.
6. Lift 3 and continue to the left side.
7. Lift 3 and weave right to the center with D.
8. Lift 1-3-4 and continue to the left.

Repeat the eight steps and insert two sticks. *(See photographs 279–282 on pages 155–156.)* The sticks may be painted with a permanent ink pen to blend or contrast with the colors in the hangings. Continue weaving the above eight steps for the length of the hanging.

See photographs 283 through 290 on pages 157–159 for other decorative ideas for your hangings.

Many of the techniques that are used in the Christmas hangings (they needn't be seasonal; they can be woven in colors that harmonize with a room and hung in corners, windows, or doorways) can be used in hangings made on warps that have all one color on one layer and all of the other on the second layer. Although not as easy to do, they are ultimately more versatile. The instructions for the basic steps for this weave follow. See illustration 34. Substitute L (light) for W (white) and D (dark) for N (natural).

1. Lift harness 1. With shuttle L weave from the left to the center. Bring the shuttle out.
2. Lift harnesses 2-4-1, reinsert shuttle L, and weave to the right selvedge.
3. Lift harnesses 1-3-2 and weave to the center from the left with shuttle D.
4. Lift harness 2. Bring shuttle D to the right selvedge.
5. Lift 2-4-3. Bring shuttle L from the right to the center.
6. Lift 3. Bring shuttle L to the left selvedge.
7. Lift 4. Bring shuttle D to the center from the right.
8. Lift 1-3-4. Bring shuttle D to the left selvedge from the center.

Using each shuttle in turn (instead of having one shuttle go in both directions before changing shuttles) gives a better interlacing of the weft shots. The cross will be one and one instead of two and two.

Note: On an eight-harness loom the first half of the warp would be threaded on the first four harnesses and the second half on the second four harnesses. The weft could then pass from selvedge without the interruption at the center. The first half would be woven on the top layer and the second half on the bottom.

278 Start weaving the hangings in the usual way with thrums. If you want a fringe, leave enough warp for it.

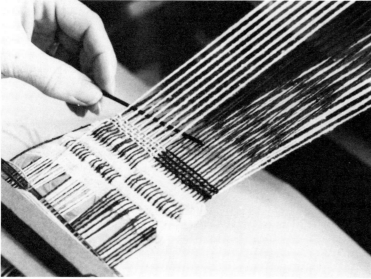

279 Lift harness 1. From the left selvedge, push the stick through the shed and bring it up through the center of the warp.

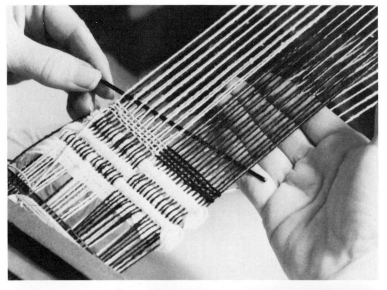

280 Lift harnesses 1-3-2. Reinsert the stick into the shed and push it through to the left selvedge.

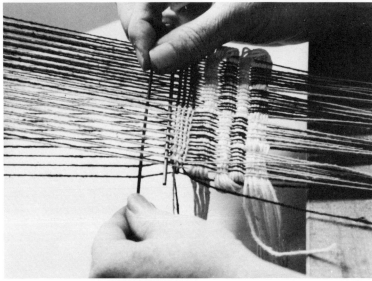

281 Lift harnesses 1-3-2. From the left, push the second stick through the shed and up through the center of the warp.

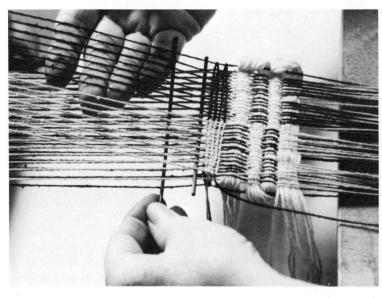

282 Lift harness 1. Reinsert the second stick. Push it through the shed to the right selvedge.

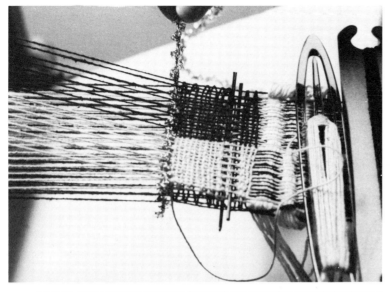

283 Silver wrapping cord is perfect weft material for a festive hanging. Use two pieces and do steps 279 through 282 for the first four steps or do all eight steps on page 154.

284 Leno adds a decorative note. Pick up the twists with a stick on the lower layer to the center.

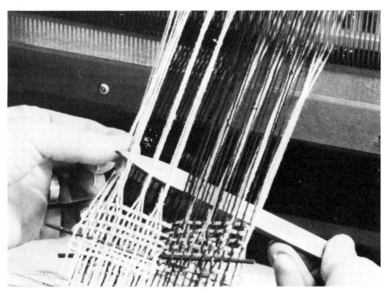

285 Then pick up the twists on the upper layer from the center to the other end.

286 Pass the shuttle through the lower and upper half layers to complete the leno. Repeat on the other two halves.

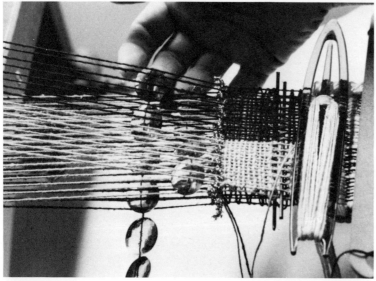

287 Strands of plastic beads can be used as filling material in the double-weave hangings. They are worked in exactly the same way as the gift wrapping cord.

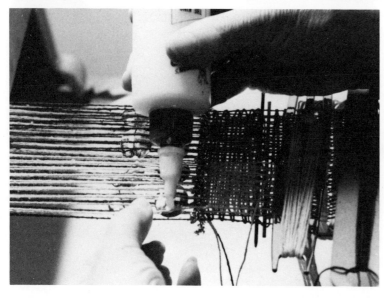

288 The beads are held in place with a drop of glue.

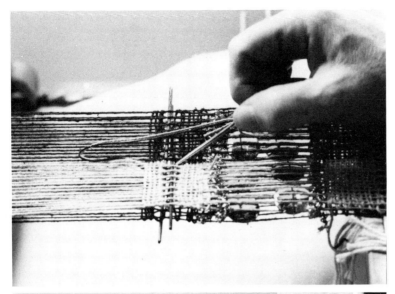

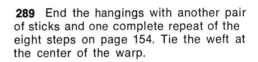
289 End the hangings with another pair of sticks and one complete repeat of the eight steps on page 154. Tie the weft at the center of the warp.

290 Leave unwoven warp between hanging projects to make fringe, which is always amusing on these ornamental pieces.

PICK-UP DOUBLE WEAVE

Hangings with pockets are very handy items. You can use them in the kitchen, office, bar, and dining room. They're easy to weave in a short time and make the most desirable gifts and sale items. For those of you who actually are thinking of earning a little money at your weaving, these hangings are much more unusual and not much more difficult to do than placemats.

When you use **pick-up double weave,** you have seamless pockets that are woven into the fabric.

The pick-up double weave is a technique that's usually used for weaving reversible patterns. No matter what the purpose, it remains the same. Once you've mastered it on the pocketed hangings, you can try your hand at wall hangings like those so popular in Scandinavia or at copies of colonial American bedspreads. Any design that can be laid out on graph paper can be woven in it. You only have to bear in mind that each square of the paper represents two warp and two weft threads.

Hanging One

The kitchen hanging *(see color photograph 30 facing page 160)* can be adapted for a dozen useful purposes around the home. The first step is to plan the pockets by laying out the things you want the hanging to hold. Do this on a piece of paper. Measure the width and length necessary to contain the items. This gives the dimensions of the warp.

> Warp: 10/2 linen, natural (N) and white (W)
> Weft: same
> Reed: 15 dent
> Sett: 15 epi
> Width: 15 inches

Make a warp long enough for several hangings. The hangings average about 28 inches in length with about 6 inches extra warp to make fringes.

The sett of 15 epi gives only 7½ epi in the double weave sections. That's sufficient for this sort of project. For the double cloth scarves *(see color photograph 37, facing page 161),* the warp was threaded 30 epi in the 15-dent reed (or two ends per

dent), doubling the number of warp threads for the 15-inch width.

ILLUSTRATION 35

PICK-UP DOUBLEWEAVE DRAFT

N				N			
	W					W	
		N					N
			W				W

N = natural
W = white

Illustration 35 is the draft for the pick-up doubleweave hanging.

ILLUSTRATION 36

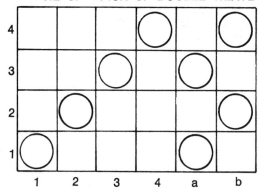

TIE UP - PICK UP DOUBLE WEAVE

Illustration 36 is the tie-up for the hanging. It can be done on a direct tie-up or table loom if it is sufficiently wide.

30 Kitchen hanging using pick-up double weave and double layer pockets.

31 Office hanging with double weave.

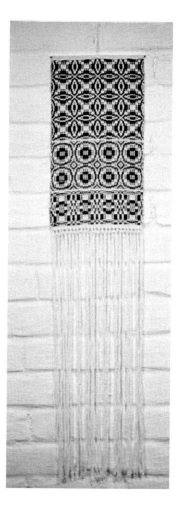

32 and 33 Reverse sides of colonial overshot sampler. Honeysuckle threading.

34 Colonial overshot cushions with a yellow warp and white weft.

35 Colonial overshot cushions. Same warp as in photograph 34 with the weft done in the same thread as the warp, with a darker strand added for highlight.

36 Skirt made on twill threading with rag, thrum, and workshop remnants for the weft. Stole done in plain weave with twill border. Both can be done on rigid-heddle looms.

37 Both parts of outfit done on a plain and green tweed yarn warp. The top uses only plain green weft. The bottom repeats warp threading in weft.

38 Placemats made on a rigid-heddle loom.

ILLUSTRATION 37

DOUBLE CLOTH

W						Top
N	N	N				Bottom
	W					Top
	N	N	N			Bottom

A.

TWO LAYERS (Reverse colors for Hanging 2)

W						Top
N	N	N				Bottom
		W				Top
N		N	N			Bottom

B.

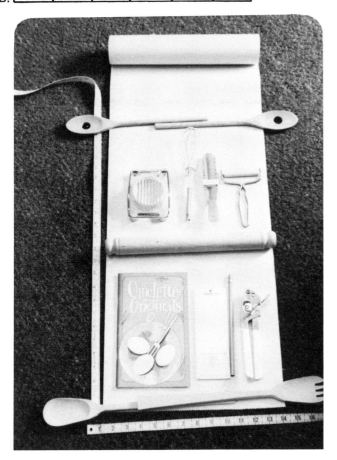

291 Plan pockets and calculate width and length of pick-up double-weave hangings by laying them out on a sheet of paper.

Illustration 37 shows the treadling order for double cloth and two layers (two of the double-weave techniques used in the hangings). They are both two-shuttle weaves. Tubular cloth, which is also used, has the same treadling order as two layers, but is done with one shuttle only and, consequently, only one color. For more information on these weaves, review Strip 4 on page 96.

Eight steps are used for all pick-up double weaves. In the following, we have used the weft colors used for Hanging One:

1. Lift harnesses 2 and 4. With a pick-up stick, pick up the design. Drop 2 and 4, leaving the pick-up stick in place.
2. Lift 1. With white weft, weave left to the right. Remove the pick-up stick.
3. Lift 1 and 3. With pick-up stick, pick up background. Drop 1 and 3, leaving the pick-up stick in place.
4. Lift 2. With natural thread, weave left to right. Remove stick.
5. Lift 2 and 4. Pick up design with stick. Drop 2 and 4.
6. Lift 3. With white, weave right to left.
7. Lift 1 and 3. Pick up background with stick. Drop 1 and 3.
8. Lift 4. With natural thread, weave right to left.

(See photographs 292 through 309 on pages 162–167 for clarification.)

Repeat the eight steps for the desired length.

292 Leave unwoven warp for fringe and weave six rows of tabby using only one of the shuttles. In this case, the white weft was used.

293 With two shuttles, weave two layers (see double weave used on Strip 4). Do not interlock wefts at the selvedges because this is going to be a pocket with side openings. Weave about two inches. Use white weft on top layer.

294 Using the white weft shuttle, close the pocket with six rows of tabby.

295 When weaving an area of tabby, carry the other weft (natural) along the selvedge by passing the white shuttle around it.

296 On the warp, lay out the objects to be held in the vertical pockets. Tie strings around the warp ends to mark the width of the pockets. Be sure to make the pockets wide enough to allow for the thickness of the contents.

There are 8 steps in weaving any pick-up double-weave design.

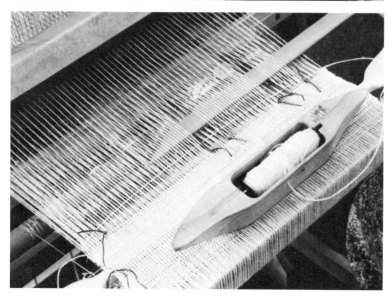

297 Lift tabby 2-4. With a pick-up stick, pick up the areas between the strings (the pockets). In ordinary pick-up, these would be the design areas. Drop 2-4, leaving the stick in place in the warp.

298 Push the stick back against the reed.

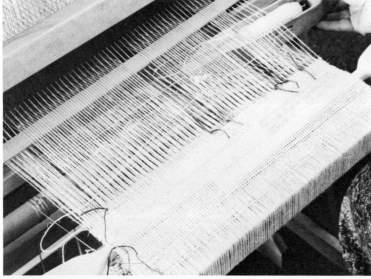

299 Lift harness 1. With the white weft, weave left to right. Remove the pick-up stick. Close the shed and beat.

300 Open tabby 1-3. With the pick-up stick, pick up the background of the design (in this case, the space between the pockets). Drop 1-3, leaving the pick-up stick in place.

301 If the warp sticks, move the pick-up stick back and forth between the reed and the web before pushing it back against the reed.

302 Lift harness 2. With natural weft, weave left to right. Remove pick-up sticks.

303 Measure for depth of pockets. They should be about ⅔ the size of the items held. Repeat the eight steps on page 154 until the desired depth of pocket is attained.

OTHER WARPS, OTHER WEFTS, OTHER WEAVES | 165

304 Above the pockets, weave on the bottom layer only. Allow for the height of the longest item to be kept in the pockets. If the pockets are to be trimmed with a fringe, insert a pick-up stick between the woven bottom layer and the unwoven top layer. Turn it on its side. Apply a thin stream of glue to the top edge of the pocket. The stick will keep the two layers from adhering together.

305 Glue can be spread with your finger or a stick to remove the excess.

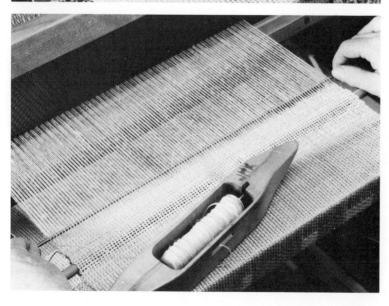

306 Repeat steps 295 through 306 for a center horizontal pocket, another row of vertical pockets, and a top horizontal pocket. Finish with four instead of six rows of tabby and place a rod strong enough to support the weight of the hanging in the next shed. Weave a few rows of tabby above it.

307 Cut the unwoven layers about three inches above the vertical pockets and spaces between them. If you do not want fringe, thread a needle with ends above pocket. Because of the shortness of the ends, it's easiest to darn the needle through the weave and then thread it than to thread and then darn.

308 The cut end will be inside the pocket strengthening it, but the needle can be easily removed through the surface.

309 Fringe may be left under the tabby rows or pulled up through the reverse side with a needle. Pull all ends in spaces between vertical pockets and between vertical pockets and selvedges to the reverse side even if you leave a fringe at the top of the pocket.

Hanging Two

If you have removed the first hanging, re-tie the warp to the cloth beam. A second hanging can be planned for the wall over a server in the breakfast room. The first hanging showed strong contrasts in color by having the light warp woven with the same color weft. In the second piece, the colors can be blended by weaving each layer with the opposite color weft.

Follow the same instructions for the first hanging to do the second hanging. The only difference is that in the latter we reverse the weft colors (W for N, N for W).

310 Two inches of double cloth are woven beneath the first horizontal pocket in the second hanging. (See Illustration 37.) The horizontal pocket reverses the order of the colors in the first hanging. (See Illustration 37.)

Hanging Three

(See color photograph 31 facing page 160.)

This hanging was designed for use near a desk or telephone in an office.

1. Start with two inches of double cloth.
2. Do two inches of leno *(see page 70 in Strip 1).*
3. Do two or three rows of double cloth.
4. Do one-inch of leno.
5. Do a few rows of tabby.
6. Use tubular cloth for pocket, approximately six inches.
7. Do not seal top with tabby. Weave only on bottom layer above the pocket.
8. Double-weave to finish.
9. Insert dowel in one shed.
10. Cut away unwoven upper layer. Leave enough over the pocket to bring a fringe back to the surface from its inside.

COLONIAL OVERSHOT

Even before the bicentennial, American craftsmen and craftswomen were looking into their collective past with a stimulating combination of pride and curiosity. The creativity of those pioneers was something to behold. With an ingenuity that approached artistry, they used whatever materials were at hand to create an indigenous tradition of crafts that compares favorably with any in the world.

The weavers were in the front ranks of these homely and courageous artisans. Almost every household had a loom. The flax (linen) was grown, prepared, and spun by the women. The wool was shorn from the sheep and taken home to be prepared for spinning. The women, thus, had their thread and yarn and were ready to release an astonishing outpouring of inspiration and beauty.

Coverlets were not only practical but also a form of decoration, a festive note in those drab and primitive homesteads. With no greater journey than to their own fields and no greater expense than the price of their own time, the weavers had the flax for their warps and the wool for their wefts. It took a lot less time than saving "pieces" from their meager supply of fabric for a quilt, and time was of great importance. Those coverlets were necessities during the long and often harsh winters.

Along with the need for warmth, there was the hunger for beauty. The "recipes" for coverlets were jealously guarded and handed down only through the family. Fortunately, there were a few generous women who traded them much as they might a recipe for home-baked bread. Instructions for favorite weaves were gradually disseminated throughout all the colonies. It is only fitting that the last new weave in *Everybody's Weaving Book* should be one of those that started the weaving tradition in this country over two hundred years ago.

Overshot provided the early crafters with a pattern that was easy to do on counterbalanced looms, the most widely used looms of the day. A twill derivative, overshot has a three-thread construction:

1. Warp
2. Pattern weft
3. Tabby

It is a reversible fabric which added a note of practicality to a period in which washday did not quite make it around on every Monday. The overshot pattern appears on one side, a reverse design is on the other. Properly woven, it is a 50/50 weave. This means that if the pattern threads were removed there would remain an even weave cloth having the same number of warp and weft ends per inch.

The *honeysuckle* pattern of overshot was selected for this book because it's a very early pattern and because it's so very pretty. Traditionally, this is done on a warp set at 30 epi, making a design unit of one square inch.

The blue and white sampler *(see color photographs 32 and 33 facing pages 160 and 161)* was woven with a 5/3 white perle cotton set at 12 epi, resulting in design units of two inches. The same white cotton was used for the tabby shots. A blue 3/2 perle cotton was used for the design shots.

Both sides of the yellow chair cushion were woven on the same warp: 1½-lea linen in yellow, set at 8 epi. The yellow linen was also used for the tabby. On one side, white wool was used for the pattern shots *(see color photograph 34 facing page 161)*. On the other, the pattern was the yellow linen with a strand of a shade darker yellow wool added for highlight. *(See color photograph 35 facing page 161.)*

The overshot draft is composed of a series of blocks. The blocks are composed of a repetition of the threading 1-2, 2-3, 3-4, 4-1 (or 1-4, 4-3, 3-2, 2-1). The pattern develops from the juxtaposition of these blocks. Obviously, the threading 4-1 4-1, 3-2 3-2, 3-4 3-4, etc. is going to result in a different pattern from 1-2 1-2, 2-3 2-3, 3-4 3-4, etc.

One of the "rules" of the overshot weave is that the weaving is done to "square the block." This means that, when there is a four-thread block or sequence threaded on the loom such as 1-2 1-2, the pattern weft is woven four times. If harnesses 1 and 2 are tied to treadle 1, you use treadle 1 four times. (The weave holds because a tabby shot always follows a pattern shot in this weave.)

But there is an exception. And the exception happens so frequently that one sometimes thinks that it is more the rule than the rule. 1-2 blocks are often followed by 2-3 blocks. That means that the weaver has to thread two adjacent heddles on harness 2. *This is impossible* because then you would not be able to make the true tabbys essential to overshot. As you will recall, they depend on a 1-2-3-4 progression. If there is a 1-2-2-3 progression at any point in the warp, the result is not tabby.

The problem is circumvented by eliminating one of the 2's at the point where the blocks adjoin. The result is that there are actually three threads to the block. If this is confusing, see Illustrations 37 and 38 on page 161 and below.

Illustration 38 shows the threading for *honeysuckle* if it were done strictly according to the blocks. Clearly, all of the adjacent threads on the same harnesses make tabby impossible.

ILLUSTRATION 38

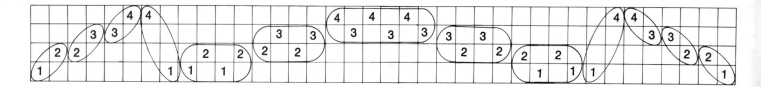

ILLUSTRATION 39

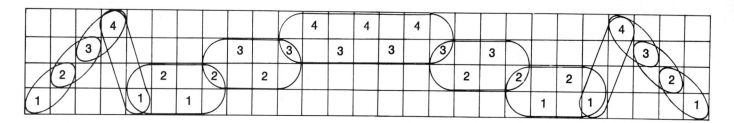

Illustration 39 shows the proper dropping of threads in the blocks for honeysuckle. Notice that between 1-2 and 2-3, one 2 drops out. It shows very clearly between the fifth and sixth blocks where 1-2 and 2-3 again follow each other. The last 2 of the fifth block and the first 2 of the sixth block form one, linking 2 between the blocks.

Another "rule" is evident in *Illustration 39*. When the direction of the progression of the blocks changes (from up to down or vice versa) as is the case in the 3-4 block, that pivot block has an odd number of ends. Because of the elliding linkage, in this case, it would result in an even number of pattern shots.

ILLUSTRATION 40

COLONIAL OVERSHOT "Honeysuckle"

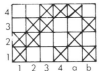

Illustration 40 gives the draft, drawdown, and tie-up for honeysuckle overshot.

Treadling orders are generally not given for overshot. The weaving remains as it was in colonial days, "as drawn in." The tie-ups do not vary but remain as they appear in Illustration 40. Treadle 1 weaves the 1-2 (2-1) block; treadle 2, the 2-3 (3-2) block; treadle 3, the 3-4 (4-3) block; treadle 4, the 4-1 (1-4) block.

Each pattern shot is followed by a tabby. An easy way to keep track of which tabby treadle to use is to have the *a* tabby always come from the left, and the *b* tabby from the right. In other words, a pattern shot from the left is always followed by the *a* tabby and from the right by the *b* tabby.

If you study the drawdown, the draft, and the tie-up, you should be able to figure out the treadling order, but don't forget those tabbys that are not drawn in because they disappear into background fabric.

Another way to figure out your treadling order is to draw the ovals (as in Illustration 39) on your draft. You know that when the ovals interlock, the pattern shots on that treadle are the same number as the threads enclosed by the ovals.

In the hanging, there are 26 pattern rows for honeysuckle. The treadling works out in the following way (although the tabbys are not listed, remember that they come after each pattern row, alternating a, b, a, b, etc.).

```
Treadle:   1, 2, 3, 4
           1 (3X)
           2 (3X)
           3 (6X)
           2 (3X)
           1 (3X)
           4, 3, 2, 1.
```

The upper portion of the blue and white sampler was woven "as drawn in" and the pattern is exactly as it appears in the drawdown. The yellow cushion was not woven in that fashion. In an effort to preserve the circles on the 8-epi warp, fewer pattern shots were used.

"Star fashion" is a term that often crops up in books on overshot. When woven "as drawn in" (or "tromp as writ"), a "star" always appears in overshot patterns. Properly woven, "star fashion" *always* has 45° diagonal lines running from corner to corner and bisecting in the center of each pattern unit.

"Rose fashion" is created by reversing the order of treadling. Treadle 4 for the 1 blocks; 3 for the 2 blocks, 2 for the 3 blocks; 1 for the 4 blocks. The result will be rounded motifs in the pattern ("roses") and no diagonals. The center portion of the sampler was woven in that way.

The bottom of the sampler was woven "on opposites." A 1-2 block was followed by 3-4 and a 2-3 by a 4-1. As you can see, the pattern had little resemblance to the original honeysuckle.

Among other things, the overlaps disappeared. A complete block was woven. When a two-thread 1-2 block is followed by a 3-4 block, two pattern shots are done on treadle 1, followed by two on 3, as every tabby follows every pattern shot. This is true whether you're doing "Star fashion," "Rose fashion," or "On opposites."

Photographs 311 through 314 give a few helpful suggestions for doing colonial overshot.

311 To bring out the pattern when the warp and weft are the same color in overshot, add a fine strand of a darker shade to the pattern weft.

312 Wool weft on a linen warp tends to pull. Use a temple to keep selvedges straight and an even width of web.

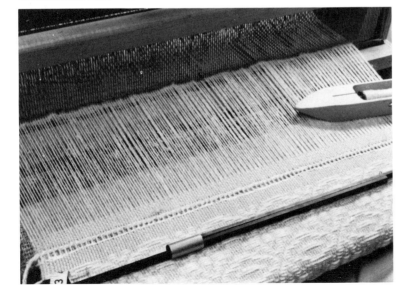

313 When weaving two projects on the same warp, separate them, after completing the first, by weaving in a heavy piece of yarn. It can be removed later to form a cutting edge.

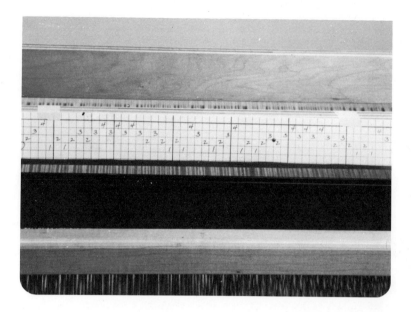

314 To keep track of the complicated treadling sequences of overshot patterns, tape a copy of the draft on or near the loom. At any interruption, stick a pin in it to mark your place.

Colonial overshot resembles all other folk art in one essential way. It was done to please the crafters. They were forever breaking the "rules." In the old coverlets, the variations in weaving and threading give an indication of how entire new patterns evolved through the years. Aunt Mary did a wheel and rose one way and came up with lover's knot. Cousin Susan did a few variations and Aunt Kate a few more. Before they knew it, they had whig rose.

The most charming name the old weavers had for this twiddling with treadling and threading was "weaver's fancy." It bears repeating. At this point you are all ready to follow your own fancy in weaving. Explore, make variations, open yourself up to the whole experience. Remember, in weaving, getting there is a good deal more than half the fun.

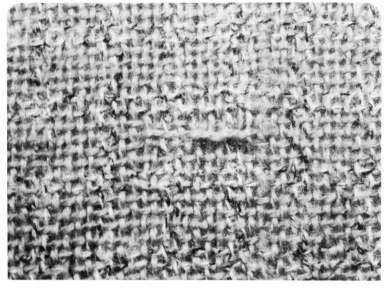

Finishing Touches

315 After weaving is completed, a misweave occasionally appears even in the work of the best of weavers. Don't be alarmed. It's simple to correct. Here we see an undesirable "float," which signals a misweave in the weft. It could also occur in the warp. The solution is the same.

316 Correct the mistake by weaving it in place with a needle threaded with the same yarn. (Using weft or warp yarn is also good for hems that won't show on finished garments or hangings.)

317 When finished, cut off the needle and thread close to the web.

318 Another unsightly thing in a finished piece is fringe that has curled from being bent over or tied to a beam. To straighten it, hold it over a pan of boiling water. Remove from steam and pull down with your fingers to speed the process.

319 Steaming will also straighten out old yarn you may want to reuse after unraveling it from a woven or knitted piece. Wind it into a skein and hold it over the steam on a wooden spoon.

APPENDIX: THE RIGID-HEDDLE LOOM
KEY TO GLOSSARY
BIBLIOGRAPHY
SUPPLIERS
INDEX

APPENDIX: THE RIGID-HEDDLE LOOM

Because the rigid-heddle loom is such an inexpensive one, it is often used by beginners and those who want to weave but cannot afford to make a larger investment. Any of the two-harness techniques described in this book can be woven on this loom. Basket weave may be a little tricky. It can only be woven very widely set. To have two threads adjacent to each other in the same shed means skipping the slot or eye between them.

With one strand threaded through an eye and the next through a slot, sheds are made by raising or lowering the rigid heddle. The thread through the eye is in a fixed position and goes above and below the slotted thread to form the sheds.

With the use of a pick-up stick, a third shed is also possible, which makes it easy to do laid-in patterns. Although it's cumbersome, picking up warp ends with the pick-up stick makes it possible to do any of the other weaves. It's simply a question of using a stick to form the other sheds. This is not the happiest way to weave, but it is possible.

Let's use twill as an example. It's an over-two, under-two weave which moves one thread over on each successive row. It can be done with a pick-up stick on a rigid-heddle loom. Because it is laborious, it's best to reserve these techniques for borders on plain fabrics such as the red border on the white stole (see color photograph 38 facing page 161). By the way, the skirt in the same picture is done on twill threading cotton warp with assorted yarns, thrums, and strips of rag for weft.

There are some special instructions for the rigid heddle that generally do not come with the loom. Because these instructions make the loom more flexible, we've added this section. Most manufacturers suggest warping the loom by bringing loops through the slot, winding the warp on the warp beam, and then bringing alternate ends back through the eyes. This makes the process sound simple and quick to do, but it works only if the warp is made of one yarn wound one end at a time.

Suppose that the weaver wants to use two ends for a special weave. Log cabin (see Strip 6) is a very good weave for this loom, but it cannot be done with the instructions that are usually included in the package. To do Log cabin, or any weave that has a warp of more than one yarn, wind the warp and thread it through the rigid heddle from the front to the back as described in Chapter 5.

For special hints and instructions on how to get greater flexibility with a rigid-heddle loom, see photographs 320 through 331 on the following pages.

320 When warping from back to front, tie a knot at the end of every two warp ends and loop them over the teeth in the warp beam. If the beam has a rod, the warp can be laced to it in one-inch bouts.

321 With masking tape, cover the warp on the beam. This prevents it from slipping free.

322 If warping from front to back, the warp can be tied in one-inch bouts and laced to the teeth in the warping beam. Again, seal with masking tape.

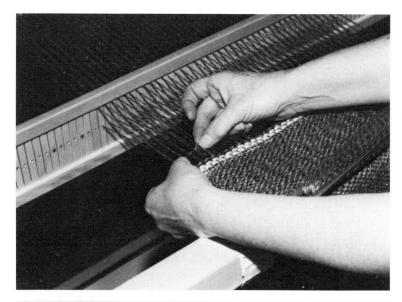

323 Weaving is done as on any loom. Start and end weft threads by turning the tails back into the same shed.

324 To make a third shed, pick up every other slot thread behind the rigid heddle.

325 Butterflies can be used to lay in a pattern under the threads raised by the pick-up stick.

326 When the pick-up stick isn't being used, you can push it to the back of the loom.

327 Overall designs can be woven by picking up ends across the entire warp. Also use this method for laying in designs worked out on graph paper.

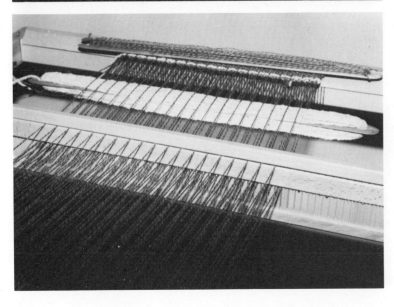

328 Rear view. The best shed is made by holding the pick-up stick against the rigid heddle.

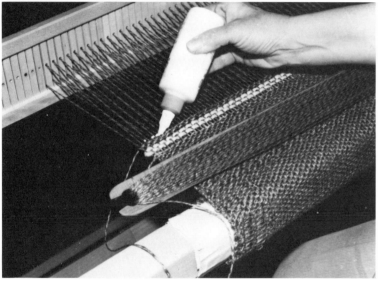

329 When the project is all finished, apply glue to the last weft shot.

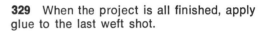

330 To remove weaving while there is still warp on the loom, weave in a strand of heavy yarn. When it is later removed, it leaves a cutting guide. Weave a few more rows of plain weave and apply glue across the warp.

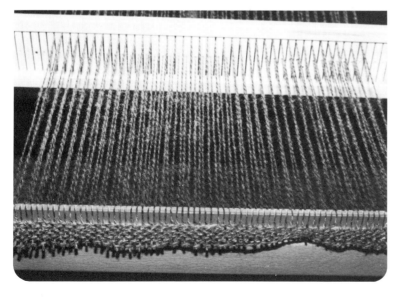

331 When the glue is dry, cut off finished weaving along the cutting guide channel left by the heavy yarn. Advance the warp, remove the masking tape from the warp beam, and place the warp over the cloth beam teeth, using the last few woven rows to hold it. If your loom has a tie-on bar, lace the warp. Do not do last few rows of weaving. Simply tie on in bouts of one inch each.

KEY TO GLOSSARY

Term	Photograph	Page
BALL WINDER	32	39
BACK BEAM	1	12
BEATER	5	14
"　　(Rug)	88	62
BOBBIN (Quill)	9, 26	15, 37
CLOTH BEAM	6	14
DENT	8	15
FRONT BEAM	6	14
HARNESS	3	13
HEDDLE	3	13
HOOK, SLEYING	8	15
HOOK, THREADING	3	13
LAMMS	4	13
LEASE STICKS	27	37
PADDLE	30, 216	38, 131
RADDLE	29	38
REED	5, 8	14, 15
SECTIONAL BEAM	2	13
SELVEDGE (Selvage)	10	15
SHED	9	15
SHUTTLE (Boat)	9	15
"　　(Netting)	10	15
"　　(Stick, Ski)	73	56
SLEY	8	15
SPOOL RACK	30, 216, 262	38, 131, 148
SPOOL WINDER	26	37
TEASEL	89	62
TEMPLE (or Stretcher)	90	62
THRUM	31	39
THREAD CLIPPER	26	37
TIE UP	4	13
TREADLE	4	13
WARP	7	14
"　　(Spaced)	8	15
WARP BEAM	1	12
WARP END, THREAD	7	14
WARPING BOARD	25, 33	37, 39
WARPING REEL	216	131
"　　"　　(Horizontal)	28	38
WEB	5	14
WEFT	9	15
WEFT END (Thread, Pick)	9	15
UMBRELLA SWIFT	32	39
YARDAGE COUNTER	26	37

BIBLIOGRAPHY

Atwater, Mary Meigs. *The Shuttle Craft Book of American Weaving.* New York: Macmillan, 1951.

Black, Mary. *New Key to Weaving.* New York: Macmillan, 1957.

Burnham and Burnham. *Keep Me Warm Tonight.* Toronto, Canada: Royal Ontario Museum, 1970.

Cavanagh, Albert. *Lettering and Alphabets.* New York: Dover Publications, 1955.

Collingwood, Peter. *The Technique of Rug Weaving.* London: Faber & Faber, 1968.

Emery, Irene. *The Primary Structure of Fabric.* Washington, D. C.: The Textile Museum, 1966.

Frey, Berta. *Designing and Drafting for Handweavers.* New York: Macmillan, 1975.

Moorman, Theo. *Weaving As an Art Form.* New York: Van Nostrand Reinhold, 1975.

Plath, Iona. *Handweaving.* New York: Scribner's, 1954.

Regensteiner, Elsa. *The Art of Weaving.* New York: Van Nostrand Reinhold, 1970.

————. *Weaver's Study Course.* New York: Van Nostrand Reinhold, 1975.

Rhodes, Mary. *Small Woven Tapestries.* New York: Charles Branford & Co., 1973.

Russell, Pat. *Lettering for Embroidery.* New York: Van Nostrand Reinhold, 1971.

Thorpe, Azalea S., and Larsen, Jack L. *Elements of Weaving.* Garden City, N.Y.: Doubleday, 1967.

Tidball, Harriet. *The Weavers Book.* New York: Macmillan, 1961.

Wilson, Jean. *Weaving Is Creative.* New York: Van Nostrand Reinhold, 1972.

————. *Weaving You Can Wear.* New York: Van Nostrand Reinhold, 1974.

————. *Weaving You Can Use.* New York: Van Nostrand Reinhold, 1975.

Encyclopedia of Textiles. New York: Prentice Hall, 1972.

Craft Horizons. Publication. American Crafts Council.

Shuttle, Spindle & Dyepot. Publication. Handweavers Guild of America.

SUPPLIERS

Here is a list of those firms whose equipment and yarns were used in the preparation of this book. For a complete international source list, we suggest that you get the *Suppliers Dictionary* from the Handweavers Guild of America: 998 Farmington Avenue, West Hartford, Connecticut 06107. The directory is updated every two years.

LOOMS

Beka
2232 Draper Avenue
St. Paul, Minnesota 55113
(rigid heddle)

Dick Blick
Box 1267
Galesberg, Illinois 61401
(Artcraft table and floor looms)

Greentree and Schact
Greentree Ranch Wools
163 North Carter Lake Road
Loveland, Colorado 80537
(floor model, rigid heddle, also carry wool, supplies, equipment)

Bexell and Son
2470 Dixie Highway
Pontiac, Michigan 48055
(counter-march)

Harrisville Designs
Harrisville, New Hampshire 03450
(floor loom kits)

L. W. Macomber
566 Lincoln Avenue

Saugus, Massachusetts 01906
(Ad-a-Harness, Jack looms)

Leclerc
Plattsburgh, New York 12901
or
L'Islet
Quebec, Canada GOR2CO
(Jack, counter-balanced, table)

Tools of the Trade
RFD
Fair Haven, Vermont 05743
(table and floor looms)

Dorset Looms
Rd L
Box 1076
Waterford, New York 12188
(portable, direct action, Jack)

Pioneer Looms
Route 4
Box 4872
Bainbridge Island, Washington 98110
(sample looms)

WARPING EQUIPMENT

Strings & Things
1402 Teller Avenue
Denver, Colorado 80215

Leclerc
(See above)

Columbine Machine Shop
1835 South Acoma St.
Denver, Colorado 80223
(electric bobbin spool winder, yardage counter)

YARNS, THREADS, FIBERS

Frederick J. Fawcett, Inc.
129 South Street
Boston, Massachusetts 02111
(linen)

Stanley Woolen Company
140 Menden Street
Uxbridge, Massachusetts 01569
(space-dyed and novelty threads)

Lily Mills
Shelby, North Carolina 28150
(cotton, plus other threads and yards)

CUM Textiles Industries
5, Koemersgarde
1362 Copenhagen, Denmark
(cottolin, wool, linen)

Berga/Ullman
Box 918
58 Demond Avenue
North Adams, Massachusetts 01247
(all types of yarns, threads, fibers, equipment

School Products
1201 Broadway
New York, New York 10001
(homespun rug wool, all other wool, equipment)

Yarn Depot
545 Sutter Street
San Francisco, California 94102
(Chenille, all others and equipment)

INDEX